Kate Walsh Slagle

# LIVE
# WITH LOSS

A SPECTRUM BOOK

Prentice-Hall, Inc., Englewood Cliffs, New Jersey 07632

S0-AKN-448

*Library of Congress Cataloging in Publication Data*

Slagle, Kate Walsh.
  Live with loss.

  "A Spectrum Book."
  Bibliography: p.
  Includes index.
  1. Separation (Psychology)    2. Bereavement—
Psychological aspects.    I. Title.
BF575.G7S57 1982      158      82-10175
ISBN 0-13-538751-5
ISBN 0-13-538744-2 (pbk.)

*To a tiny blue bird*
*who taught me much about living with loss*

This book can be made available
at a special discount when ordered in
large quantities. Contact:
Prentice-Hall, Inc., General Publishing Division,
Special Sales, Englewood Cliffs, New Jersey 07632.

1  2  3  4  5  6  7  8  9  10

ISBN 0-13-538751-5

ISBN 0-13-538744-2 (PBK.)

Editorial/production supervision by Denise Hoover
Cover design by Jeannette Jacobs
Manufacturing buyer: Cathie Lenard

*Excerpts from* Death and the Family: The Importance of Mourning,
*by Lily Pincus, are reprinted by permission of Pantheon Books, a
Division of Random House, Inc. and Faber and Faber Limited.
Copyright ©1974 by Lily Pincus. Excerpts from* Getting Well Again
*by O. Carl Simonton, M.D., Stephanie Matthews-Simonton, and James
L. Creighton, are reprinted by permission of Bantam Books, Inc.
Copyright ©1978 by O. Carl Simonton and Stephanie Matthews-
Simonton.*

Prentice-Hall International, Inc., *London*
Prentice-Hall of Australia Pty. Limited, *Sydney*
Prentice-Hall Canada Inc., *Toronto*
Prentice-Hall of India Private Limited, *New Delhi*
Prentice-Hall of Japan, Inc., *Tokyo*
Prentice-Hall of Southeast Asia Pte. Ltd., *Singapore*
Whitehall Books Limited, *Wellington, New Zealand*

# Contents

# Preface

Life is a circle of beginnings and endings. This book deals with endings that appear in the form of loss, and beginnings that grow out of living with and through major life losses. This book is about loss and grief and how to live with and through them.

It is a book for all people—individuals, counselors, therapists, anyone who wants to learn how to deal with the painful losses inherent in living.

The point of this book is to provide avenues for surviving all types of traumatic loss. A framework for looking at loss and a formula for living with it are given as a means for doing this. By means of the *framework,* which can be thought of as a clear window, we can more vividly understand loss and its journey into grief, symbolized here by the evolution of a rainstorm, with its attendant thunder and lightning. The *formula* supplies us with the ingredients to provide us a safe passage through each phase of the storm.

Highlighting this book is the perspective of grief as a process of unfolding. Within each described stage of grief, exercises are presented to facilitate easier movement through that particular phase.

A perspective of balance is offered—the pain of loss and grief, as well as the richness and growth that follow—to illustrate that living with loss is two-sided.

One unique and vitally important concept explored in this book is unresolved grief and the dangerous directions in which it can travel. Signs that warn of unresolved grief and methods for dealing with it are examined.

Evolving out of my personal losses and gains, this book also weaves tapestries of loss and grief through the shared experiences of others who have been through it and can show us the way.

This book is about the cycle of life. On one side of the coin is loss—its pain, devastation, and grief. On the other side are gain, growth, and insight. Where there is loss there is gain, and where there is gain there is loss. And so turns the wheel of life.

I would like to acknowledge some very special people in my life who came to my rescue to help me type. Thanks, Marji, Cathy, Jackie, and Scarlett. And thanks to Heather, Margaret, and Cindy, whose loving feedback was so invaluable.

I'm very grateful to the courageous people who so willingly and openly shared with me their struggles with loss: Bobbi, Bill, Louise and Dewey, Marji, Darlene, Mike, Betty, and Jack.

And thanks to Rudy for being my anchor.

# THUNDER AND LIGHTNING

Watching the clock inch its way from 2:25 to 2:30, I was mesmerized by the drama of the big black hand's jerking movement every time the red hand came full circle. So much for attentiveness to Latin II. The theatrics of the clock was so much more interesting than Gaul being divided in three parts. I was fifteen that day in November, a high school sophomore trying to survive the tedium of learning Latin, a dead language. Hoping that time would pass faster if I studied the movements of the clock, I noticed the crackling sound of the P.A. system filling the room. That seemed strange. We still had 31 minutes until the final announcements from the office signaled the end of another school day. "Ladies and gentlemen, we've just received a news bulletin." The faceless voice shook as it took in a deep breath and continued. "The president has been shot." We all seemed to gasp in unison. "Word on the president's condition is not known at this time. Please take a few minutes of silence to offer a prayer for our president." At 2:50, the voice in the blonde-colored speaker exploded with the news that President Kennedy had been shot in Dallas and had died.

The country was left in a state of shock and confusion on that day in November. Some people wandered around as if in a daze, while others covered their faces with their hands and cried. Almost everyone who was old enough to remember that day can cite specific details of what they were doing when they heard the tragic news. Why is this? The loss of this young and vital leader stunned an entire nation. Lives were shaken. Fear reigned. That day, seeming at first like any other day, became deeply etched within the national memory. The instant the news was heard, people across the land felt a jolt. Breath caught in their throats, as their bodies jerked from the impact of the blow. It was much like the reaction to thunder when it crashes directly overhead and resonates throughout the entire body. Thunder rumbled throughout the country on that fateful day.

Thunder is like loss. Both occur in nature. Thunder and its accompanying storm are natural phenomena; loss can be seen in nature as the rising moon changes into the dawning sun, as day slips away into night.

Thunder is like loss. The similarities can be seen in three specific ways in which they impact our lives: both have a jarring effect, both are like thieves, and both scare us.

## THE JARRING EFFECT

Thunder jars the softness of a still night. Loss jolts the calm pattern of our everyday lives. Our nation was rudely shaken by the news of the death of the president, and the pattern of our daily routines was altered. It is no wonder that the day is so vividly remembered.

A crash of thunder is usually accompanied by a flash of lightning, which, in a moment of suspended animation, briefly illuminates the world outside our window. Flashes, recollections of past losses from my own life shed light on the jarring effect of the thunder of loss.

*It is late on a Saturday night. I'm working as a counselor at a crisis center. Finishing my shift, I'm completing my paperwork. Something is happening. I notice a slight headache above my right eye. "I'm probably really tired. It's been a hectic night," I think calmly as I take off my glasses and rub my eyes. As I begin to write again my vision is blurred. The words on the paper are appearing animated, moving in waves up and down the page. Fear tightens in my chest. "It's really nothing. I'll be all right," I say to myself in an attempt to calm down. It's probably better not to dwell on it. I'll get my attention on something else. Rudy should be here any minute to pick me up." Another counselor has just entered the room. I'll distract myself with conversation. "Hi, Sandy. What's new?" I ask, trying to maintain a sense of normalcy. She is talking and as she relates the new events in her life, I'm realizing that I'm somehow not here with her. Trying to respond and make contact with her, I'm aware that the words just will not come. I see them in my head but they seem to get lost before finding their way out of my mouth. I'm feeling as though there is a short-circuit in my brain. The fear is rising again, tension in my chest, constriction in my throat. I'm breaking into a light sweat. I'm feeling split in two. One part of me is smiling and nodding at Sandy, acting as if everything is all right, and another part of me is pleading for this loss of control to go away.*

*A knock at the door. It's Rudy. I'm relieved. I'll be safe now. I relax, feeling rescued. As we're driving home I'm aware that it is not over. I'm locked up in my body. I can't communicate to him the fact that something is wrong. The desire is here, the thoughts and words are here, but damn it, they can't find their way from my head to my mouth. Rudy is telling me about a TV show he saw tonight. I nod my head as if I'm listening, while inside I'm beginning to panic. I know I can't. A voice deep inside guides me. "Do your deep breathing—easy now—in through the nose, out through the mouth. Relax—stay with it. You're going to be okay—just stay with the breathing—that's it, easy and deep." Finally a passageway opens. The words come tumbling out. My body is working right again. "Something is wrong with me, Rudy. I'm feeling kind of strange." Again the gap. The words are not coming out. My face has a prickly sensation. My head seems unattached to my body. "What's wrong?" questions Rudy. I shrug my shoulders and gesture in a way that indicates that I don't know. Once more I do the deep breathing, regain some speech, and tell him that I'm feeling funny inside, that something strange is taking place. We're home. I feel more secure here. I'm doing some yoga postures and working with my breathing in an attempt to relieve the anxiety that fills me. I'm beginning to feel better now. The sweating has stopped. I'm calm. My speech has returned and my head is once more on my body. I'm aware of being extremely careful not to alarm Rudy. If he gets scared, then so will I. Now that I'm sure that I'm no longer in physical danger, I'm relating the whole story to Rudy. He says I should see a doctor. Since I'm back to normal, I decide that it was just some sort of bizarre reaction to stress and not enough rest.*

Denial has always come easy for me. So I tucked this frightening experience away and put it on a shelf, next to a dozen other experiences tagged "To be forgotten."

*It is six weeks later and we're out feasting on steak and lobster. Sitting here in the restaurant, I look at the wall and notice a block of darkness. Must be the lighting in here. Focusing on the cloth napkin on the table, I observe that I can see only part of it. The other part is a big black spot. I break out in cold beads of perspiration, and clamminess engulfs my body. My face tingles. I'm not going to say anything. If I just ignore it, then it will go away. I still have my speech, so everything is fine. I'll make light conversation. On our way home the left side of my tongue becomes numb. This can't be happening. It's all in my mind. The numbness is spreading down my left arm and into my hand. I must be having a heart attack. No, that's ridiculous! I'm only twenty-seven years old. I'm scared. I need to stay calm. I'll do my breathing, it worked last time. Something has got to be wrong. I've got to stay calm. Once I get home I'll feel better. Breathe. At home now, I'm mumbling to Rudy about not feeling well. Again I do my yoga, concentrating on relaxation. As I begin to relax, I feel the tingling sensation that comes as numbness leaves and feeling returns. There, I'm feeling better. Now it's safe to tell Rudy. He insists that I see a doctor. "Okay, okay, I'll go to the student health center tomorrow."*

*The next day, relating these strange symptoms, I sense that the doctor's reaction is not as nonchalant as mine. She's ordering a complete physical along with neurological tests. I don't understand what the big fuss is all about. I feel fine now. A few days later the diagnosis. I feel like I'm being sentenced to limbo. I learn that it's either that those damn birth control pills that I take are causing the blood to form clots in my brain, or there's the possibility of multiple sclerosis. She's explaining that the symptoms are similar. They strike at different times, leave no apparent damage, and disappear as suddenly as they came. This can go on for years until the disease advances to a stage at which it can be detected. There is no cure. The Crippler of Young Adults—that's ironic. I remember as a kid going door to door collecting money for research on multiple sclerosis.*

I had no emotional reaction to any of this. Living in my head with the whole thing, I kept myself objective and detached, as if I were watching a movie of something that was happening to someone else.

*It's been a few weeks now since my visit to the doctor. I'm running 3 miles every day, going to class, doing my regular routine. Nothing has changed. Everything is the same. Working on the crisis lines, I'm untouched by my own crisis going on inside. I'm talking to a woman. She's called before and has told someone that she's dying. Today she's hedging around that fact. She's throwing out clues about not being well, but is attempting to focus on less intense topics. I'm understanding that she is denying the reality of what is actually taking place in her life. It's as though someone else were talking as the words pour from my lips. "I know that you are dying and I understand that you may not choose to talk about that now. But denying it will not make it go away." I can't believe I've said that. She's screaming now—a loud, piercing scream that seems to be streaming out from her guts. God, did I blow it? The scream continues. Did I say something wrong? As painful as the scream sounds, I somehow believe it's healing. It's okay. I must allow her the room to vent. It appears that all of this has been locked up inside her for a long time. The screams are dying down to painful sobs as she shares the tale of her disabling disease. Of how she's tried to ignore it for three years. Of how she's carried it all inside alone, not able to tell her children or her sister. She's saying it isn't fair. She's not even thirty yet. The tears are running down my face as I share the incredible pain, anguish, and anger with this woman about her death. Now she's exploring the possibility of getting some help in dealing with all these feelings. The call ends and I am totally drained. I feel as though I'm walking around in a fog, feeling numb all over as if I were in shock—floating, as though my feet were no longer rooted to the earth. Everything seems unreal to me. Talking about the call, I am attempting to shake this unnatural feeling that is haunting me. I'm telling another counselor how I really felt this woman's pain. "No, that was your pain you were feeling," she answered. It's like being slapped in the face. What is she saying? That can't be true. My knees are about to give way as the heaviness of this truth sinks into my consciousness. My whole being is stunned, shattered. My denial is no longer intact. All of my buried feelings about the possibility of having M.S., a life-threatening disease, are beginning to churn and bubble deep inside. I am feeling deep shock. Other truths are beginning to surface. My life will never be the same. I know that now. I can no longer carry the heavy burden of those bottled-up feelings. I'm at a turning point in my life. These feelings about M.S. are just the tip of what I've accumulated and tucked away for many, many years.*

Loss is an inevitable part of the flow of life. No one is immune to loss. The thunder of the loss of my health jarred my life and shattered the calm, everyday routines I had once had. My life would never be the same again. Both thunder and loss jar our lives.

## THUNDER AND LOSS AS THIEVES

Thunder and loss are as thieves. Thunder steals away the peace and quiet of the night. Loss robs us of the wholeness of our lives. The loss of President Kennedy took away peace and contentment of a nation and left, in its wake, a sense of imbalance and emptiness. Understanding what loss is shows us how the thunder of loss steals away the wholeness of our lives.

### What Is Loss?

Loss is connected to beginnings and endings. In Eastern philosophy there is the concept of "t'ai chi"—a circle divided into two parts, representing opposites—light and dark, *yang* (male) and *yin* (female).[1] It embodies the idea that the whole, the circle, is made up of polar opposites. A day consists of light and dark. A year contains both winter and summer, hot and cold. A river is both passive and active, yielding and strong. In the whole of life there is both loss and gain. Where there is loss there is gain, and where there is gain there is loss. Together they make up the complete circle.

Change, in Eastern thought, is seen as the continuous flow of one polar opposite into the other and back again. Nature illustrates this concept. The seasons change from blasts of freezing winter winds to the aromatic breezes of spring, from the stiffling stagnant heat of summer to the crisp, fresh air of autumn, and back to the cold blasts of winter. These changing seasons constitute the whole, the complete circle that is called a year. Within this whole, the year, loss and gain co-exist. Each season is lost to the next season, which is gained and then lost to the next. Changes that occur within the cycle of human life contain these same opposite elements. Change implies the end of one thing and the beginning of another. Change is made up of losses and gains, endings and beginnings. Both polarities are present. A major life change is retirement. Within this whole event are the elements of both loss and gain. There might be the loss of a structured, 40-hour work week; the loss of camaraderie with fellow workers; the loss of the "breadwinner" role; the loss of a job; the loss of substantial income. Intertwined with the losses could be gains: unstructured time that is all one's own; the opportunity to develop hobbies and interests that there was no time to pursue in the past; the freedom to relax or travel; a new self-image; a different source of income.

Since both loss and gain are inherent in this life change, how is this event perceived? Whether the change is considered as a loss or a gain depends on what the individual values. Imagine life symbolized by a circle—complete, whole, continuous. Harmony flows between our inner world of thoughts, feelings, values, and our outer world of external events and experiences, as we feel a sense of "oneness" or "centeredness." As a major life change occurs, an ending and a beginning, our circle is disturbed. Some things are lost and some things are gained. If we value what was lost more than that which was gained, then there is an empty part in the circle; it is like a pie in which a piece has been cut away. The size of the missing section of the pie is dependent upon how much value we placed on the loss. The more we valued what was lost, the larger the empty part in the circle. The harmony of our inner and outer world is thrown off-balance. The wholeness of the circle is broken, and we feel a sense of being "off-center." The change is experienced as loss. Going back to the example of the person who retires, if that person values the structured time, fellow workers, the "breadwinner" role, the actual job, the income—in short, the losses—more than the gains, then the change of retirement is experienced as a loss. If the retiree values the gains from retirement more than the losses, then the retirement is viewed as a gain; the circle is enlarged. Again the continuity of the person's life is upset. Even though the gains are positive in nature, they cause the circle to grow larger, and this brings imbalance into the person's life. The wholeness of the circle is broken.

Likewise, if what is lost and what is gained from a life change are of equal value to us, the circle stays whole; there is balance. Neither loss nor gain, but a combination of both, a sense of bittersweet, is experienced. So change is encountered as loss or gain or both, depending on what is most valuable to the individual.

Since each of us is unique and different, what we value also varies. Values are made up of belief systems and the investment of the self. Belief systems are what we are taught to value. Some people are given messages that hard work and frugality are valuable, while others learn that loafing and extravagance are valuable. The amount of ourselves—our time, energy, feelings—that is invested in a particular person, place, or object will determine its value for us. Since we each give differing amounts of ourselves into varying activities, interests, and people, we place certain values on certain things. So what *I* experience as loss may not feel like loss to *you*, and what *you* perceive as loss may not be loss to *me*. A flash from my life illustrates this.

*I'm sitting in the school cafeteria, choking down hot coffee. It's a cold, wet day. I'm feeling devastated, as if I've lost my best friend. Shivers are running up my legs from my sopping shoes. My parrot is dead. He was like a best friend. He kept me company while Rudy was overseas. When I first got him as a Christmas present, he was so wild. It took six months for him to understand that I wouldn't hurt him. I'll never forget the first day he finally trusted me and landed on my shoulder. God, how funny he was when he imitated the alarm-clock buzzer! He gave me so many hours of joy and laughter. He loved spaghetti. Now he's gone. I didn't know how much he meant to me till now. I'm trying to tell the people at this table why I'm pale and teary-eyed today. Stan understands. He's not saying a word, but I feel his caring as he strokes my hair. Steve is across the table, looking perplexed. He's opening his mouth to speak. "I can't understand why you're so upset. It was only a pet bird." My heart is sinking. There's no way you can understand.*

Since I invest a large part of myself in pets, they become very valuable to me. I loved my parrot; I *valued* him. He filled a large section in the circle of my life. When he died, a big chunk of that circle was stolen away. My wholeness was broken. I felt a gap, an empty spot in my life. I experienced loss. Steve, whose value system did not include giving parts of himself away to animals, could not understand how I suffered such loss over a pet bird. What was loss to me wasn't loss to him because of the difference in our value systems. So what is loss? Defining it based on the concept of change is not possible because of the diversity in human values. But loss can be defined in terms of deprivation. Loss is being left without something valuable that we once had.[2] Thunder and loss are like thieves. They steal away the peace and the wholeness of our lives.

## THUNDER AND LOSS SCARE US

Sudden, loud thunder paralyzes us inside as a result of the childhood memories of other storms. Buried memories of long-ago losses freeze fear within our hearts. The loss of this country's beloved leader to an assassin's bullet in Dallas, Texas froze fear in the hearts of this nation. How is it that loss scares us so? Theories of loss point to a possible answer.

## Theories of Loss

We sense a feeling of loss in reaction to change. Changes in human beings begin at birth. Moving from life inside the warm, protected womb to the new, unknown world outside is one of our first experiences in coping with loss. Other losses in infancy have been studied by a number of theorists. Alexander Lowen, in *Depression and the Body*, provides a summary of the loss theories of Karl Abraham, Melanie Klein, and René Spitz.[3]

"Primal depression in infancy"[4] is a concept formulated by Karl Abraham. This type of depression is thought to be rooted in the child's experience of a loss, the loss of mother's love. This early feeling of loss comes from situations in which the infant feels deprived because a basic need is not being met. A small baby experiences love through being fed, held, rocked, and kept dry and comfortable. If these needs are not answered, the baby perceives a loss of mother's love. Crying out in protest and rage, the instinctual feelings of loss, the baby senses further withdrawal and rejection if the mother, for whatever reasons, is still unable to satisfy these needs. Eventually, the child learns to shut off the expression of these feelings of loss and withdraws into depression. Abraham relates adult depression to this type of early loss in infancy. It may be that the reaction to loss in the adult is a backlash of feelings aroused by similar circumstances of deprivation in infancy.

Melanie Klein believes that the sense of sadness, fear, and abandonment sometimes seen in the expression of a preverbal baby represents the "infantile depression position."[5] This behavior is seen as a response to the threat of the loss of mother's love. In Klein's opinion, the threat of being deprived of love arouses feelings of hostility toward the mother, who is loved and whose loss is feared. These early, frightening feelings of ambivalence, love, and hate toward the same person create a dilemma within the child. To cope with the threatened loss, and to restore security in the midst of ambivalence, the child internalizes a permanent mother. If the child experiences withdrawal, rejection, or absence, more than a warm, nurturing presence on the part of the real mother, the "internalized mother" will be "bad" rather than "good." The ability to tolerate loss in later life, Klein maintains, rests on this early process. "Melanie Klein sees success at establishing a 'good' object in early childhood as a precondition for the ability to tolerate later anxiety about loss and separation,"[6] says another writer.

The loss of physical contact with the mother and its effect on the children were studied by René Spitz.

He observed the behavior of babies separated from their mothers after six months of life because their mothers were in penal institutions. In the first month of separation, the babies made some effort to regain contact with a mother figure. They cried, screamed, and clung to anyone who was warm. As these attempts to restore their lifelines to feeling proved unsuccessful, they gradually withdrew. After three months of separation their faces became rigid, their crying was replaced by whimpering and they grew lethargic. If the separation continued, they became more withdrawn, refused contact with anyone and lay quietly in their beds.[7]

John Bowlby probed the effect of separation from the mother figure on babies between the ages of 6 months and 30 months.[8] The child's reaction to separation, according to Bowlby, seems to go through three phases. In the first phase the infant protests the loss, crying and screaming in anger for the lost mother. In the next stage, that of despair, while feelings of hope appear to burst forth from time to time, the baby gradually loses interest in his or her attempts to recover the mother. The final stage, that of detachment, shows the child as withdrawn and depressed. Bowlby expanded on Klein's position—that the child's internalized "good" mother is a prerequisite for the ability to tolerate later loss—by emphasizing the idea of "separation anxiety" in early childhood as the main key in understanding an individual's reaction to loss:

> Separation anxiety expresses dread of some unspecified danger, either coming from the outside or from mounting internal tension, and dread of losing the object believed capable of protecting or relieving one. The baby's first response to this threat is protest and screaming; followed by, if the threat is not removed, withdrawal, apathy and despair. Separation anxiety will be reactivated in all subsequent fears of losing a person to whom a deep attachment exists.[9]

Abraham speaks of loss in terms of retriggering the "primal depression of infancy," while Klein stresses the "infantile depression position" as the primary response to the threat of loss, with an attempt to internalize the mother as a resolution of the loss. Spitz observes that if separation from a mother figure continues beyond 3 months, the infant gradually withdraws from everyone. Bowlby documents the three phases in the child's reaction to separation from the mother, and introduces the concept of separation anxiety in early childhood as the means for understanding the reaction to loss in later life. The main thread weaving through these various theories of loss is that adult reactions to loss seem to be based on experiences with loss that took place in infancy and early childhood. What do these theories tell us about loss? Loss is an experience that starts early in life. And growth, for human beings, seems to be connected to the way we cope with early experiences of loss.

A flash of lightning shows my way of dealing with an early loss:

*I'm six years old. My family is very large and close-knit. There are six of us kids. We live with our parents and grandparents in a rambling old house on the east side of Dayton. My grandparents grew up in Italy. They talk funny sometimes. I'm the fourth oldest. It's Saturday night and we're watching the "Wonderful World of Disney." Grandma is in her rocker. Grandpa sits in his white vinyl high-backed chair. Ma is in the kitchen boiling hotdogs. Pa is still working at the grocery store down at the corner. All of us kids are lying on the floor in front of the TV. My world feels warm and secure. We're all laughing at Donald Duck sputtering away on the screen in front of us. I stop and listen and suddenly realize that Grandpa isn't laughing—that's not laughter—it's some kind of strange, scary noise. I've never heard a noise like that before. Grandma is out of her chair standing over Grandpa. She screams, then cries out in Italian. She is slapping his face, shaking him, crying and screaming in a language I don't understand. Horrible choking sounds are coming from Grandpa's throat. I'm on my feet. Ma is running in from another room. Someone is shouting, "He's dead, he's dead!" Grandma is sobbing. I am frozen in terror. I cannot move. I'm looking at Grandpa. He's still now. His face is an odd color. The word "dead" rings in my ears. I'm trying to shut it out with my hands. Everyone is in motion. There are loud voices shrieking. I'm confused, terrified, shaken. I need to get away. I run—escaping to the farthest corner in the kitchen. There's an old cardboard case where Pa keeps his beer bottles. Weak-kneed, I stumble onto it and resting my head on the cold green wall of the kitchen. I shake and cry, as I desperately try to sort out in my head all that has just taken place. I feel alone. This scares me the most, as I try to hide—away from it all.*

No one is immune to loss. I grew up pretending to be the exception. For me, my grandfather's death was marked "To be forgotten." Loss was still something that happened to other people, but not to me.

Loss, like thunder, startles us and steals from us. But why does it frighten us so? Loss has been hidden away in our society and, like anything that's been locked up in dusty attic rooms, it becomes dark and foreboding. The aim of this book is to take away some of the fear of loss by presenting a framework that will help us deal with loss and a formula that will allow us to live with loss.

## THE FRAMEWORK

Why do we need a framework, a special "window" through which we look to see loss clearly? Loss is not something that is shared openly in this society. Since its reality is hidden in the dark, since it is denied in our culture, we replace it by illusions or myths. The main illusion that we carry concerning loss is based on the notion that everything in our lives—people, places, objects, events—has permanence. We maintain this myth by the mechanism of denial. One way we deny is by convincing ourselves that we are somehow immune to loss. Loss happens, but only in the lives of other people. No one is immune to loss. Yet we all pretend. Lightning struck once again in my life and again I tried to pretend.

*I'm twelve. It's a holiday—a Holy Day of Obligation. That means that as Catholic schoolkids, we get the day off from school. I play the piano. I've been taking lessons for four years now. The nun who teaches me knows that my Grandma is Italian. I guess she wants to get on her good side because she teaches me songs like "Santa Lucia" and "O Sole Mio." Grandma shares my love of music. There are eight of us kids now, and getting noticed in this crowd is pretty tough. But Grandma notices when I play the piano. She slips me a dime when nobody is around and tells me to keep it our secret. Then she asks me to play and she sings along. I feel important and happy and special with our shared secret. I feel close to her.*

*This morning I'm up early and at the piano by 8 o'clock. Ma is sewing in the next room. The other kids are scattered between the kitchen where they're eating, and watching television in the living room. The piano is by the stairway leading upstairs. I've been enjoying myself, lost in the music, for about an hour. "Kate, stop playing—I think I hear Grandma," calls my mother from the dining room. I stop, listening, waiting. No sound comes from upstairs. I'm playing again. It's 9:30 and I'm sensing some kind of tension in Ma. I hear it in her voice as she asks Bobbi, my oldest sister, to go up and check on Grandma. Bobbi says she will, but is straightening up the house as if to avoid going upstairs.*

*It's been a while now, and I'm tired of playing the piano. Since Ma is sewing, maybe she'll take time today to teach me to sew with a pattern. I've been after her to do that for weeks now. As I ask her, I'm aware that she seems distracted, as if she's not there, as if her mind is thinking about something else. She mumbles something about Grandma not being down for breakfast yet. Her face is lined with worry. She's up from the sewing machine and is heading upstairs toward Grandma's room. I'm following. She's opening the door with me on her heels. I'm pleading my case for why today would be a good day to teach me to sew, when I catch a glimpse of Grandma out of the corner of my eye. Something registers as being wrong. Her eyes are wide open, but she isn't seeing. Her mouth is dropped, but she isn't talking. Her hair looks as though it's standing on end. She is so very still. Ma is shaking her, calling out her name. Grandma stays very still. I leap down two flights of steps and stand panting at the bottom. Ma is in her bedroom phoning our aunt who is a nurse. I hear her end of the conversation. "I think mom is dead. No, there is no pulse. I didn't have time to check. I know that she's dead. Okay, and hurry."*

*I'm frozen, quivering all over. I run—out the front door. I'll go next door and get our neighbor. I'm spending the rest of the day here at Mrs. Lee's. Away from my house, away from death, away from my loss. Later, I overhear that the coroner placed Grandma's time of death at 9:00 in the morning—during the time I had been playing the piano and Ma had heard her call out. I'm stunned. I'm alone. I'm in hiding.*

Each time loss struck my life I hid, trying to deny the reality of it. I kept holding on to the idea of permanence, trying to deny the reality of loss, trying to push away the fact that loss is a part of life. Another illusion that we maintain about loss is that if we don't feel its pain, then it won't be real. I tried really hard to stay numb to loss, as you can see in the following flash.

*"Hi, Eleanor, are you ready for your tour?" We're on our bikes and I'm showing my new friend, who just moved into the neighborhood, all the sights and highlights of Carlisle Avenue and surrounding territory. She's really pretty—dark-haired, bright blue eyes, shining teeth. I really like her. She's friendly and warm and kind of shy like me. I know we're going to be the best of friends. We're in the same class at school. We delight in sharing the fact that our teacher is the craziest nun in the whole school. They call her "the sex teacher," because all she can talk about is sex. Eleanor and I both turned bright pink the day she separated the girls from the boys. She took us all in an empty room and told us not to wear tight sweaters because our breasts would be growing. She showed us how to walk with our shoulders hunched forward to hide our budding womanhood so we wouldn't tempt the boys. It felt neat to be sixth-graders, sort of like being grown up. I can imagine Eleanor and I double-dating on our first dates.*

*It's been a week and Eleanor hasn't been in class. Guess she has the flu that my sister Treeny just got over. I'll have to go to her house. Feels empty without her in the seat next to me. Weird Sister Adrian is starting class. I wonder what she'll come up with today? Wait a minute. What? She's saying that Eleanor is in the hospital—she's going to die—from something called leukemia. No! My stomach feels like it just dropped down to my toes. I'm numb. My chest is so tight I can barely breathe. I feel like something's been cut out of me—from my guts. I feel so empty. My head is reeling.*

*Once a week now, Sister is giving us reports on Eleanor. Another of our classmates is in the hospital to get his tonsils out. Sister says that he and Eleanor have been playing cards together. How come Johnny and that strange nun get to see Eleanor and I don't? I'm her friend. It's not fair. I don't see why I can't go to the hospital just because I'm not sixteen. What a dumb rule! You have to be sixteen to visit your best friend in the hospital! Somebody told me that they made that rule because of younger kids carrying too many germs or some dumb thing like that.*

*Eleanor died today. Why doesn't that nun just shut her big fat mouth. I don't want to hear that Eleanor was in terrible pain at the end. I don't want to hear that as she died she bled from her eyes, ears, nose, and mouth. Everything inside me is screaming. "No, not Eleanor—it's not fair—she's my age—people don't die this young—she's nice and pretty and damn it, she's my friend!" Our class is at her funeral. I won't believe she's dead. I never got to say goodbye.*

*We're back in our classroom. A few days have passed and the routine is resumed. Our crazy teacher has sent down to the first-grade classroom for Eleanor's sister. Can't she leave well enough alone? Here she comes. God, she's so tiny. She looks so much like Eleanor. Can't this nun see how scared she is? Her little body is trembling. Why is she making this poor little kid stand up in front of forty sixth-graders and tell them about what her dead sister had been like? I can't take this. My hands are gripping the desk. My knuckles are turning white. I'm holding myself down in this desk, struggling to keep from screeching what my whole body is feeling. "You big witch—leave her alone—leave me alone. Stop this!" But I'm keeping it locked inside, simmering, boiling. All the pain of losing my friend, all the anger that death got her too, all the rage at that nun for acting as if Eleanor isn't a real person. She's giving the little girl a Holy Card and is patting her on the head. I must pretend that I feel nothing. Otherwise, I'll rip that nun apart. Calm down. Put this away. Don't feel. There, now I'm numb again.*

Each time loss occurred, I stuffed my feelings about it deep down inside. Staying numb was my way of not accepting loss. I carried the notion that if I did not accept loss, it was not real.

Our myths and illusions cloud our ability to accept loss as a fact of life. They are used to deny its reality. So loss becomes something to be locked away in closed-off rooms. But when something is hidden, it becomes bigger and more ominous. It takes on more power, and becomes more frightening. It becomes something to hide from so that it won't get us. Consequently, we are unprepared to deal with loss when it does come into our lives. That is why we need a fresh perspective, a way to approach loss so we can look at it openly, in the sunlight, without fear. Looking at it as if through a clear picture window will help to prepare us for dealing with loss.

Seeing loss as a natural part of the cycle of nature, like the development of a thunderstorm, will make it easier to accept and live with.

What is the framework? It is the clear window through which we can see and understand our illusions about loss. We will follow the process of loss as though watching the evolution of a summer's thunderstorm.

Chapter One is entitled "Thunder and Lightning." Thunder represents loss. Lightning is the metaphor for my own personal experiences with loss. In this section we'll look further into loss as well as introduce the first ingredient in the formula: Learning to give yourself permission.

Chapter Two is "The Storm." The storm symbolizes the process of grief. Using the window to look into the storm, we'll see theories about grief, a model of the process, cultural attitudes that surround grieving, and the second ingredient in the formula: Creating an atmosphere of trust.

Chapter Three is called "The Mire." The mire is the symbol for getting stuck in grief and the consequences that follow. Here we will learn the third ingredient in the formula: Flow.

Chapter Four completes the circle and takes us to "The Clearing," an image of clarity, gain, and growth. Within the clearing we will see the transformation of loss and gain, growing through grief; we will learn what living with loss means, as well as looking at the final ingredient in the formula: Creating a climate for opening.

Thus, we will look at loss and its journey into grief through a clear window. Now let's take a look at the four-ingredient "formula" that will enable us to pass safely through each phase of the storm.

## THE FORMULA

Why do we need a formula for living with loss? With loss hidden away in this culture, we don't have any guidelines for learning how to live with and through it. We're taught to numb ourselves to the feelings of loss. I learned early that my feelings of loss would be invalidated by the world. I learned to hide my tears. To feel them and show them in public was somehow considered weak. I learned this unwritten, unspoken law early in my life.

*Ma is telling me to get ready for bed because I have to get up and go to school tomorrow. I'm busy watching Bimbo, my pet parakeet. He seems to be having trouble keeping his balance. He keeps falling off his perch and his eyes don't look right. "Ma, I think he's sick," I say. "Don't worry," she says, "he'll be all right. Now go up and get ready for bed." The next morning, I bounce downstairs all dressed and ready for school. Going through the dining room on my way to eat breakfast, I look in the bird's cage. Where is he? Oh no—he's lying on the bottom, perfectly still. "Mom," I scream, "the bird is dead!" The tears are coming uncontrollably now. I'm sobbing, choking on the tears. My chest aches with pain. Ma holds me for a few minutes and says it would be best if I go on to school. I don't want to go. I hurt too bad. I can't eat. Still, I swallow the tears, do as I'm told, grab my books, and walk over to school. I'm trying hard to pretend that I don't hurt.*

*I'm sitting in the basement classroom, in second grade, distracted by the pipes that run across the ceiling as I try to do my arithmetic. We're practicing writing the number 2 in our workbooks. Pictures of Bimbo, lying stiff and still on the bottom of his cage, keep popping into my head. My eyes keep filling with tears. I wipe them away so nobody will see. I continue drawing the endless 2s, filling each page. I gaze up at the pipe, and see my bird lying on the bottom of his cage. The tears are rolling down my cheeks. I'm embarrassed. I try to choke them back. The harder I try to hold them back, the more noise I make. Gulps are escaping from my throat. Sister Mary Paul has me on her lap, asking me what's wrong. I'm sobbing now as I spit out the words; "My bird died." My chest is heaving as the pain pours out. I feel Sister tighten. My nose is running all over the place. I feel forty pairs of eyes riveted on me. But, try as I might, I can't stop. Sister is telling me that everything will be all right. "After all," she says, "it's not as bad as if your Grandpa had died." Little did she know that Grandpa had been buried almost a year earlier. Now she's handing me a tissue and a Dr. Seuss book. She tells me to read it so that I'll cheer up, stop crying, and feel better.*

When feelings are invalidated, the message is that they are not important, that they don't matter. I was learning early to bottle up all my feelings.

I stayed with the illusion of being immune to the pain of loss. I kept myself from feeling until something happened that caused a hairline crack in my armor, as lighting struck again.

*I'm a senior in high school. It's the day of our mid-term exams. The principal is making the daily morning announcements. In an all-girls' Catholic high school the morning prayers are followed by announcements about the kinds of trouble some of the girls have been into and stiff warnings to the rest of us. Carla, my cousin, cohort, and classmate, has just been called out of the room. I wonder what kind of trouble she has gotten herself into this time. "Anita Amato, a former alumni and sister of Carla Amato, has died this morning of cancer," rang the words over the loudspeaker. Oh, my God–it's Anita. She's twenty-four years old. She's had cancer for about a year. We knew this was going to happen, but I still can't believe it. Anita, my older cousin. We'd gotten to know each other this year. Listening to Peter, Paul, and Mary and Joan Baez in the basement. Talking–all the time talking and laughing. She was opening up a whole new world to Carla, Lyndy, Judy, and me. She was an adult we would talk to, not like our parents. She never judged our ideas, she just listened and gave us her thoughts. She filled us in on family gossip that we'd missed because we were too young. Now she's gone.*

*Here comes Carla. She's white and pale, and is picking up her books. Maybe I should go with her. I can't move. She looks like she needs somebody right now. I'm paralyzed. I'm scared to go with her. Carla has left. The bell is ringing as I stumble out the door to take my journalism exam. I feel really out of it–disoriented–as I'm caught up in the sea of blue uniforms flowing down the corridor, bits breaking off like so many small rivers into various classrooms. There's Judy. Tears are pouring from her eyes. Up ahead is Lyndy. Her eyes are blood-red. We silently join together, hug each other, and continue on to the hollow classroom for our test. The knot in my throat is melting into drops of liquid that overflow from my eyes onto my face. I should feel ashamed, embarrassed, crying openly like this in front of all these people. Lyndy and Judy aren't ashamed, so neither am I. Besides, this feels relieving. I never knew it could feel so good. We're sitting together, the three of us, sharing tissues and tears, trying to see and concentrate on exam questions through a thin veil of water. It's hard to think. Images of Anita keep flashing through my mind. I can see her in the hospital making us all laugh to cover up her pain and to ease our discomfort at not knowing what to say. I can see Carla's white, ashen face, bravely picking up her books, with a look of pain ready to break just beneath the surface. I hurt. This time I hurt too much to hold it inside.*

I had always conned myself into believing that if I ran and hid, the feelings—the pain, anger, guilt, and tears—would not find me. I thought they'd just go away. But I was wrong, they didn't. They stayed deep inside as I began to lose my ability to feel, my humanity. To keep a firm grasp on our precious humanity— this is another reason that we need a formula for living with loss, so we can remain human, so we can remain alive.

Each ingredient in the formula for living with loss will help us to pass through each part of the thunderstorm. We will examine each of these ingredients in greater detail later. Skills will be taught along the way to help facilitate passage through the thunderhead. The formula will provide guidelines for living with and through loss.

---

"Black Friday," said the commentator on the 6 o'clock news, describing that cloudy day in November on which a nation lost its leader to an assassin's bullet. It was indeed black, because an entire country had been wounded and left in shock and pain. Walking to my locker, as if in a bad dream from which I couldn't wake, I felt the hushed silence that hung in the usually boisterous halls. The pep rally had been canceled. There was no pep. People wandered, as if they were in a trance. Inside, I felt numbness grip me. Some eyes rained tears. "Black Friday" said it all as I made my way home, feeling as if threatening dark clouds loomed overhead. Thunder seemed to rumble in the distance.

Thunder is like loss. Earlier, we saw thunder and loss as jarring occurrences, as thieves, as frightening goblins. They mirror each other in three additional ways: They wear different faces; they are chaotic; and both bring warnings.

## DIFFERENT FACES OF LOSS

Thunder comes to us in different ways. It wears different faces. Sometimes it shows itself by crashing directly overhead, jarring our windows and jolting the very foundations of our homes, as if it were the face of impending doom. At other times the thunder just rumbles ominously in the distance like a big lumbering bear, moving all around us yet careful not too come too close. Its effect on us is not the same. Loss wears different faces, too. Some losses strike close and are profound, while others touch our lives in a lighter way. Just as thunder is experienced differently, with its different faces, so it is with loss.

## Types of Loss

Losses come in different shapes and forms. Some losses are expected, while others descend upon us without warning. Some losses may happen as a result of a conscious choice, while others seem to be beyond our control. Losses may intrude upon our lifespace suddenly, or they may appear gradually. They may arouse intense emotional reactions, or feelings of only minor irritations and annoyance. The types of loss are numerous, but they can be divided into ten major categories: the loss of a loved one, the loss of some part of the "self", the loss of valued objects, age-related losses, symbolic losses, limbo-state losses, geographic losses, career losses, network losses and seasonal loss.

### Loss of a Loved One

Louise and Dewey had four children, all daughters. Their youngest child, Jennifer, had been born with many physical difficulties, including jaundice, an enlarged heart, and hydrocephalus. She was not expected to live for long. But the doctors didn't know Jenny's strength. She not only lived, she got better. Her enlarged heart eventually returned to normal size, the jaundice disappeared, and the hydrocephalic condition improved. Her body began to grow.

Later it was discovered that Jenny had severe scoliosis with attendant early hydrocephalis, a condition that made it impossible for her to even hold her head up. The doctors said that she would never walk, that she would never talk. They told Louise and Dewey that she was retarded and they shouldn't expect any more from her. But the doctors didn't understand the miracle of Jenny or her family. Knowing the reality, that Jenny was going to do whatever they thought she was capable of doing, the family decided to help her reach high expectations. One of her sisters taught her how to walk. Christmas came that year as Jenny took her first two steps down the hall. The girls showed her how to chew gum, and when she learned to chew gum, she discovered how to chew food. The love and encouragement of her family helped her to move toward realizing her potential. The retardation was minimal, she was walking in a brace for the scoliosis, and she was talking. The school district was considering placing her in a regular kindergarten class. All her obstacles were being overcome. She was growing. She was catching up in spite of all her physical problems. She was attending a preschool program. There wasn't anything she wouldn't try. She was a cute, gutsy child, and everybody loved her. Jenny's life looked bright and promising when she was struck with leukemia. She was five years old when she died, when her family lost her.

One of the most agonizing losses experienced by human beings is the loss of a loved one. The most profound way that we lose our loved ones is through death, as in Louise and Dewey's loss of Jenny. This kind of loss is staggering, leaving the survivors emotionally wounded and bleeding.

The loss of loved ones also occurs as a result of divorce, separation, or ending of a friendship. The loss may be the permanent end of a relationship or a temporary ending. In whatever form this loss takes, it brings enormous and lasting changes into our lives. Things are never the same again.

The loss of a loved one does not always have to be connected with the loss of a person. Many of us invest a part of ourself in our pets. As time and energy are given to the care, feeding, and training of an animal, and as the pet responds with affection and loyalty, a relationship built on a bond of love and trust is formed. In this way a pet becomes a loved one. So the loss of this kind of a trusted friend, especially if the animal was perceived as an important member of the family unit, can be experienced as a traumatic loss.

### Loss of Some Aspect of Self

Betty, a woman in her forties, experienced a loss of a part of herself as her children began to become more independent and needed her less. Her role in the family began to take on some drastic changes. She describes her loss of her role as "mother."

*When the oldest of my four children reached adolescence, I experienced a deep depression, one that I was unable to counter in any of the "usual" ways. I felt useless and energyless and just worthless. Telling myself how great a cook, seamstress, mother, hostess I was simply didn't work, because for one thing, I just did not believe it, and for another, I didn't care that much about being a great any one of those things anyway. I spent days smiling my kids and husband out the door in the morning, and then bursting into tears when I turned to face an empty house. I had so longed for this time when all the children would be in school (my youngest was in first grade) and here I was crying the day away. But I really didn't think I was in trouble with it. I knew I felt bad, and that I felt bad about myself, but it was nothing that a new interest or a good cry wouldn't set right, sooner or later. Then, volunteer work in the elementary school wasn't as much fun as before. In fact, I didn't want to do that any more. I took long walks that October, my hands clenched into fists, so I wouldn't lose my hold on sanity, and the tears streaming down my face. Sometimes, those long walks included involved fantasies—here comes the widow, the victim of that awful tragedy when her husband and all four children were wiped off the face of the earth. Oh, those were good for lots of tears—tears of sorrow when I was most deeply into the daydream, and tears of guilt when I'd ask myself why I chose that particular theme. I never had an answer, except to decide I was going crazy. Eventually, the pain was so great that I thought most anything would be better than going on this way. I began to think very seriously about throwing myself off the top bunk while I was making it, or of deliberately stepping on the wet soap when showering. I thought I wanted to be taken care of, and that those would be good ways to insure that. I said to my friend that I was just so tired of taking care of people. Just so tired of being used. So tired of being mother. She often reminded me of how fortunate I was to have such a gentle husband. I would agree but I didn't really want to hear that—it just made me feel guilty. For a long time, I kept a tape I made from the depths one night. In a tear-soaked voice, I was asking why I needed to go to the schoolyard in order to feel "special." I had no answer. After a particulary bad month that spring, when I came very close to a suicide attempt, I got plugged into a mental health program and began seeing a counselor. One of his suggestions was that, you guessed it, I get involved with some volunteer activity to help fill my time with constructive activity. I actually applied for and was accepted in the suicide prevention program. That was a nice boost for several months, but by the next summer, I was seeing the old pattern beginning to emerge again, and I went to another counselor. This one asked me what I wanted to do. Out of the blue, I told her I wanted to go back to school and get a degree. She said, "Why not?", so I did, got a B.A. in psychology, and an M.S.C. in counseling and a lot of good strokes about my helping skills. Even began seeing some clients. Maybe even helping a few. Then, one day I was reviewing a session with a client. I realized what had happened to me. All that verbiage about how tired I was of being a mother. All that garbage of how tired I was of being used. All that smoke to help me deny a really big pattern. Ever since I was a child, when I felt rejection of any type coming on, I, in effect, picked up my marbles and went home. What happened to me, although I surely had no idea at the time, was that I realized that a very consuming facet of my identity was in danger of evaporating. My youngest was in school all day. My "oldests" were in adolescence, and really testing the waters, and I was losing my identity, my reason for living. My claim to fame. Myself, myself, myself.*

Losses that are not quite as obvious include the loss of some aspect of the "self." The self is the complete mental picture that each of us holds about our body and personhood. Betty was aware that something was wrong in her life, that something was missing. Since this type of loss is not so readily apparent, it can take a while for a person to get a handle on it. In Betty's case, it was a few years before she began to understand what had taken place.

This loss of some aspect of the self encompasses the loss of confidence, ambition, personal power, the loss of a way of feeling about ourselves, the loss of identity, the loss of health, and the loss of a familiar, secure role.

Another example of the loss of some aspect of the self can be seen when a person loses his or her health due to illness or disease.

Bill, a twenty-three-year-old man who believed he was healthy one day and the next underwent surgery that removed 2 feet of his intestines, lost an additional part of himself when he discovered he had to live with a chronic intestinal condition called Crohn's disease. Weakening the lining of the intestines and perforating them, the disease progresses into peritonitis. At this point, the affected area must be removed. There is no cure, and Crohn's does not remain in one place. It skips all over the body, and cannot be controlled. With the loss of his health, changes were forced into Bill's life. Choices were taken away, such as what foods he could or could not eat. Since eating was one of his pleasures in life, he felt robbed, as if someone or something had done him wrong. Bill was told that during those times when the disease flared up, he would have to have complete bed rest. For someone who had so recently thought of himself as a young, vital, active person, this restriction dramatically altered Bill's lifestyle.

He experienced embarrassment at having this disease, having to turn down food that was offered him, then having to explain that he had a disease in order not to hurt his hostess' feelings. He began to not like himself very much. He had changed. His life had changed. He lost the way he used to be. Angry and depressed at first, he felt bitterness toward anyone who came near. He felt that his world had ended. And in a sense it had. His life as it had been, eating the foods that pleased him, feeling good, being free of pain, speeding around doing what he wanted to do when he wanted to do it—all of that was gone. The quality of his life, as he had known it, was missing. A way of being was gone, a part of him was lost. His "self," the person he had thought he was, was gone.

Locked within this loss of "self" are feelings we carry about who we are, about what are our unique qualities, our capabilities, our worth, and our attractiveness. Through his disease, Bill lost the person he used to be; he felt worthless and unattractive as his mental picture of himself began to change through the loss of his health. He experienced this type of loss as he was learning how to live with this illness.

### Loss of Valued Objects

Marjie had driven home from work as soon as the kids called to tell her someone had broken into the house. When she arrived and surveyed the damage, the bedroom seemed to be the disaster area. Looking at the destruction, she felt furious and nauseated. She felt as if she had been violated. Someone had entered her private bedroom and ruined everything in sight. The room was turned upside down, every drawer and closet emptied. And it all lay in water from the slashed waterbed. Unable to walk into the room, Marjie called the police. As she went through her jewelry box items, realizing exactly what was missing, she felt angrier and angrier and started crying and shaking. Her diamond ring, which had been given to her by her deceased grandfather eighteen years earlier, was gone. The diamond had been a part of her grandmother's Eastern Star ring. One diamond had been given to each granddaughter— five of them. And now Marjie's was gone. The police arrived and made a report. They were cold and uncaring.

They told her that missing items are only rarely found after a robbery. The worst part of it was that she knew who had robbed her. The ten-year-old down the street had broken in twice before; it seemed clear that he was the culprit this time too. Her ring was just down the street, and there was nothing she could do.

Marjie just sat on the couch at first, sobbing hysterically and feeling as though she might explode with anger. Life seemed to go on around her as if nothing at all had happened. The kids wanted dinner, the phone rang. She felt paralyzed with pain, and so enraged at being violated that she couldn't speak. She felt like murdering, rioting, and screaming. She couldn't believe that there was nothing she could do about it. She found it difficult to accept the idea that she was supposed to just sit there and be a good citizen, when what she really wanted to do was to go down the street, slash tires, break windows, and get her ring back. It meant nothing to the thief, but to Marjie it was a piece of her grandfather, a gift that he had given her, all she had left of him. So for the rest of the evening she just sat, immobilized. She never recovered what was stolen, and doubts that she ever will. The ten-year-old is older now, and still lives down the street. She can't even look at him. The anger is still with her. The sadness has melted into a dull pain. She still hurts. She still looks for her ring at auctions and in junk shops. She even still looks for it in her jewelry box.

This is another form of loss, that of valued objects or property, such as money; the loss of a home through fire, flood, or other natural disasters; the loss of a car in an accident; the loss of homeland; or, as in Marjie's case, the loss of valued possessions like family heirlooms.

### Age-related Losses

Age-related losses are those that happen as a natural consequence of growing into and through the different stages of life. Here, a thirty-six-year-old woman shares the experience of an age-related loss, which she experienced following the breakup of her marriage; it was the loss of her childhood.

*During the first few months following the breakup of my marriage, I began to feel some new feelings I'd never had before. I felt totally alone, with no one to rely on. I had never felt this way before. There were always my parents—even while I lived away from home at school. They were there, or I felt they were there if I needed them. After getting married, there was my husband for support, for caring and warmth and protection. Now, with no marriage, or husband, I was thirty years old and feeling lost, alone, and scared. I even had children I was supposed to care for. And no one to care for me! The feelings of being alone were overwhelming to me. I felt anger that no one, not even my parents, had told me that this is what it was all about to grow up; no one had prepared me for this real isolation. It was clear to me—it even screamed in my head—"It's you, only you. You stand alone. You take care of yourself. No one else will." Those feelings are not as overwhelming now, six years later, but they are just as intense at times. I don't easily accept losing my childhood and gaining my adulthood. Six years ago my therapist said, "So now your balloon has popped. Now what?" And that is exactly what it was—my toy broke, things were not the same. I lost something that was precious and important to me. Now what?*

Other losses of this type include leaving home for the first time, loss of teeth, hair, youth, beauty, as well as the loss of childhood.

### Symbolic Losses

Human beings use symbols to stand for things that they hold dear. The American flag has been a symbol of the ideals on which this country was built. A symbolic loss is the loss of a valued symbol. The turbulence and social unrest of the 1960s caused many people to encounter losses of this nature. Ideals, values that we were raised to believe in, changed as public opinion about the war in Vietnam and our government's involvement there came under scrutiny. With the Civil Rights Movement, the Poor People's March on Washington, and the War on Poverty, the very structure of our form of government came into question. For many, the experience of being in the military during this era changed perceptions, ideals, and values about themselves and their country. As old symbols disintegrated, new ones took their place. Men with long hair became symbolic of change as the validity of the stereo-typed "male role" was challenged. The 1960s passed into the 1970s, a time of noninvolvement and re-evaluation. Again, the symbols changed, and again symbolic loss was experienced.

Mike was a veteran of the Vietnam War. Leaving the military, he made the decision to let his hair grow. His long hair came to symbolize different things for him. On one level it was a form of rebellion and a reaction to his experience in the armed forces. On another level, having felt depersonalized as a soldier, his hair came to be symbolic of his assertion of his uniqueness, his individuality. For eight years his hair grew. With the war well behind him, and after some years in college, Mike came to the realization that in order to be assimilated into the job market upon graduation, he was going to have to cut his hair. He didn't just go to a barber. He felt that he needed care taken as he gave up his symbol. So he went to a hair design salon, and spent fifteen dollars to have a beautician cut off his hair. She really didn't do anything different than a barber would have done, but Mike felt that this would ease the blow, that somehow the cutting would be less painful, that more care would be taken if it cost more. But that didn't help to ease Mike's sense of loss. His hair was gone. He felt as if a part of him were gone. He described a physical emptiness in the pit of his stomach. He felt powerless, as if there were nothing he could do, as if something were irretrievably lost.

He felt angry at the system—angry because he had had to give up this symbol that meant so much to him. He felt angry that he was judged by the length of his hair rather than by who he was. He felt pain, emptiness, and frustration. He felt loss.

Peretz, in his article "Development, Object Relations and Losses,"[10] points to a variation of this type of loss. Institutions can also be symbols and this type of loss is called *institutional loss*. Loss of faith in the government, or form of government, changes in education, changes in religion, and changes in the family structure are all examples of this kind of loss.

### Limbo-state Losses

Sue was working on automatic, just to get her six-year-old daughter to the hospital. For the next eight hours she was in a state of shock. Everything seemed to be moving very slowly. All motion and direction was very deliberate, an almost dreamlike quality to it. There was a wall of haze, a fog bank that separated her from what was happening around her. Yet afterward, she remembered every minute detail of the experience. She refused to deal with the possibility that Mary was dying right there in front of her, or that she might survive, but in a vegetable state. Sue remembered Mary crying "Mommie," looking for her when she was right there in front of her. She remembered the nurse whispering to the doctor that she was losing the pulse and vital signs, as Mary lapsed into a coma. She recalled the doctor screaming into the phone for a brain surgeon, *now*. She remembered walking with the stretcher down to the operating room, and listening to the brain surgeon as he explained what could go right and what could go wrong. She remembered touching Mary and looking at her very carefully for perhaps the last time that she'd be alive, as they wheeled her into the elevator marked "Surgery." She and her sister waited out the long hours of surgery. They laughed. They joked and made fun of the ducklike walk of the pediatrician. They giggled as they sneaked down forbidden hospital basement halls. They sat, and then they walked because they couldn't sit any more. And then they sat because they couldn't walk any more. They joked and conversed about everything else except Mary. Because they had to. Because if they hadn't, the waiting would have been intolerable. Sue didn't want to think about the "what if's" and yet she considered every single possibility. She didn't want to discuss what was happening, and yet she called each and every family member and talked about it. Time was moving in slow motion until the surgeon walked through the door. Then it felt, for Sue, as if everything had moved too fast. She didn't feel ready to hear what he was going to say. She just wanted to run, to leave, and to not listen.

Some life events produce a feeling of suspended animation. In *How to*

*Survive the Loss of a Love*, Colgrove, Bloomfield, and McWilliams refer to this kind of loss as a "limbo-state loss."[11] It is a time of waiting, a time when the outcome is unknown. The not knowing induces a sense of loss, just as we witnessed with Sue awaiting the outcome of her daughter's surgery. (Mary did survive the surgery and now is a healthy nine-year-old.) Other situations that can involve limbo-state losses include awaiting the outcome of medical tests or the results of a licensing exam such as for the bar; having a friend, relative, or spouse "missing in action"; and the time space after a lovers' quarrel. The limbo state is a loss state in which the person is left hanging in mid-air.

### Geographic Losses

Michael had lived in the house for a total of four and one-half years. He rented it from his father and uncles, who were the owners. It had been his grandfather's house. Since it wasn't a profitable piece of property, the house was finally sold and Michael received word that he had to leave. For him, it was a sad time. He had grown attached to the old place. He'd put a lot of himself there. The house was not in good condition so Michael had fixed it up, paneling the bathroom, putting tile in the kitchen, using materials he had scrounged together. Another reason the house held meaning for him was because he'd lived there as a child when his family first moved to California. He'd been six years old, and this was his grandparents' farm. He had memories of going out and gathering eggs with his grandmother in the chicken house, and playing with all the animals on the farm. It had been a time full of richness for him. He had lived in the house another time, after the breakup of a relationship. His brother was living in the house at the time, and Michael stayed there with him for several months. It was a warm, secure haven for him during a time of conflict and confusion. It was a home. A few years later when his brother moved, Michael had taken over the place. It was his home now. And it seemed to have a personality all its own. For example, the sink trap was really a radiator hose because the sinking floor made the pipes so crooked that the regular sink trap wouldn't fit. It was the little things like that that made the house special and unique. On moving day, Michael felt sick inside, as if a part of himself were being displaced. He felt sad, as if he were leaving a dear friend. He had been very connected to that old house because of the times of growth that he'd experienced there. And now he was leaving some of that behind. He gazed for a long time at the place, and felt the need to apologize for leaving his old companion to the fate of the bulldozer. It hurt to leave. He felt as if he were abandoning a childhood friend.

Our society is a mobile one. Job transfers from one end of the country to the other are commonplace. Changes of residence, for a variety of reasons, happen to us quite frequently. With these changes come losses, as we saw with Michael's experience. These are called geographic losses, and they include changing jobs from one sector of the country to another, changing schools, and moving from a home.

### Career Losses

Jack owned his business. He was a private investigator. After fifteen years in this work, however, Jack found himself becoming bored, restless, and easily fatigued. He wrestled with bouts of depression. Frequently, he realized that he was lost in daydreams. Slowly, he began to let his business go, avoiding attending to work tasks by finding other things to do. If there was a book or magazine lying around, he'd pick it up and read, whether he was interested in it or not, as a way to avoid dealing with the business. One day he began to understand the problem. He realized that he wanted out of the work he was doing. But he found himself paralyzed, unable to take the steps to make a career change. One of the things holding him back was the "shoulds" that he was placing on himself. They grew out of the values and expectations that he had been raised with; he found himself thinking, "You should want to stay in this job. It was your chosen career and if you leave it, then you have failed." He felt that he was probably immature because he was a forty-year-old man who didn't know what he wanted to be when he grew up. Leaving a career that he had outgrown was causing him conflict because that was against the rights and wrongs he had been taught. And yet he wanted out. He needed to be out. The way he dealt with his ambivalence was by involving himself in other unrelated activities that took his time and energy away from dealing with this conflict.

Once his business fell apart, Jack began to submit resumes, and ultimately got a job in a totally different field. After settling into this new career, he started to feel the loss connected with this change. Part of this vague sense of loss had to do with giving up something that was familiar. It may not have been giving him the satisfaction that he needed, but his former business had been safe. So Jack experienced a loss of that security as he moved from the known into the unknown. He realized that there were parts of his former career that he missed, such as the freedom of being his own boss, not answering to anybody. He missed the unregimented time structure of his other career; now he worked from 9:00 to 5:00 every day. Jack was letting go of some of his past in this job change and for him, the letting go was the most painful part of all.

More and more, change is becoming a lifestyle of this culture. Not only do we change locations more often, we also change careers more frequently. Thirty years ago when people chose an occupation, they were likely to remain in the same line of work for the entire span of their work life. Not so today. In the current job market, career changes happen as often as every five years. Jack, who had been taught in the old school, experienced a great deal of conflict with the idea of a job change. Change can happen so rapidly that the old values don't catch up. People get caught in that space in between, so changing occupations can be a traumatic loss.

Other career losses include being fired from a job, being promoted or upgraded in position, or experiencing a change in a former area of work.

### Seasonal Losses

Some of us experience seasonal losses when, for example, summer changes to fall, or after vacations, or at holidays like Christmas, and birthdays. This is a loss that I've experienced.

> It's October—that same old time of year again when I get to feeling empty, down, and listless, breaking out unexpectedly in tears—over what? There's nothing bad happening in my life right now. Besides, I seem to get this way every year, no matter what's going on. My birthday comes this month, but I'm not sad because I'm a year older. Wait a minute—I know why I'm down. I'm flashing on the bright colors of autumn leaves in Ohio—hot apple cider—the crisp smell of fall at this time of year. Fall doesn't seem the same in California. I remember the birthdays in Dayton, when I was a kid—the warmth and security, the closeness of me and my eight brothers and sisters, the cake with the candles on it and twenty people gathered in song at that long table—it always reminded me of the "Last Supper." All those people who are so close to my heart are still in Ohio—and I'm out here without them. This is the time of year when all my feelings, longings, yearnings break through. I miss them. I'm feeling the loss of each and every one of them.

### Network Losses

A major loss can carry with it a network of losses. The act of rape is a violent assault on the body and psyche of a woman which robs her, not only in a physical sense, of her very personhood. This senseless, brutal attack is followed by a network of losses: the loss of the body, and within that is threaded the loss of confidence, self-respect, self-image, security, the loss of normalcy and stability in the space of the woman's life, the loss of family and friends, and the loss of illusions.

Bobbi recorded her dreams. She began stirring, drifting back to consciousness, and rolled over to write down a dream that she'd just had. It was about a man and woman walking, or something, and the scene suddenly shifted to the man drowning the woman, and she was struggling. As Bobbi reached across the bed to pick up her journal, she felt the blows coming from nowhere. There wasn't any pain, just shock. It was like blows of electricity running through her. Reality just wasn't registering. It was all happening too fast. By the time she was hit again, it started to become real for her, too real. Someone was in her bedroom beating her. And then she passed out. When she came to, it was with the thought of survival in mind. Her instincts took over as she turned her head into the pillow to protect her face. She remembered putting a hand up and catching a painful blow. She heard herself yelling, "Stop hitting me! Do what you want!" And the thought passed through her mind that it was her own fault for leaving the patio door opened. It had been stifling in the apartment, and the cool night breeze had felt refreshing; it had seemed like a good idea at the time. The man stopped hitting her and squashed the pillow down over her face in an attempt to smother her. Bobbi knew she was dying. She had run out of breath. Instinctively she began fighting and struggling. She freed her face and shouted over and over, "I can't breathe!"

The smothering ceased. He kept the pillow over her head, but allowed her to breathe. He never said a word. He just held the pillow down with one hand and began to unzip his pants with his free hand. Bobbi got the impression of something being set down. It was the weapon he had been beating her with. He pushed her legs apart with his knee and he started to rape her. Bobbi was intent on surviving this brutality. She tried to pretend that he was the man that she was currently seeing, but she couldn't make it connect. Everything slowed down for her. Time seemed distorted. The sexual act seemed to take an eternity. And yet her mind was moving fast. She wondered if she'd be mutilated or murdered. She decided that if she was lucky she'd live through it. In that case she'd need some evidence to prosecute. It was as though she stepped outside herself as she tried to reason a way out of this. She scanned her options, and short of murdering him, saw no guarantee of her survival. Killing him was ruled out as she realized that he was a whole lot stronger than she. She thought about her daughter Tracy, who was spending the night with a friend—what if she should return home unexpectedly? She considered screaming. She felt trapped in her own bed with a maniac on top of her who might or might not chop her into little pieces. She imagined a slow death. This guy had to be crazy, she reasoned, so he'd get pleasure out of her slow torture. With this possibility in mind, she decided to go along with whatever he had in mind so as not to rile him, or set him off.

Her mind skipped to trying to figure out who this was, who she had been in contact with lately. She remembered hearing somewhere that most rapists know their victims. Who was violent and bizarre enough to be assaulting her like this? All at once she knew it was a young man. And then it connected. Instinctively she knew. This was Duane, an acquaintance of her daughter. She didn't see his face. She didn't have to. And something deep inside told her not to look. She remembered hearing that sometimes you can talk a rapist out of it. But again the voice inside told Bobbi not to open her mouth. Her feeling was that he was not "wrapped up too tight." She sensed a coldness, a deadly lack of feeling from this person. To attempt to appeal to his sympathies, when he didn't have any, seemed like a fatal mistake to her. Now her mind had skipped to the concept of a God that was supposed to protect women from brutal idiots like this. Where was he now? She felt cheated, betrayed, let down. Why wasn't he striking this guy down with a bolt of lightning? she wondered. No magic came, no lightning bolts, no knight in shining armor. She felt abandoned. Gradually, she felt grateful because she was still alive. He hadn't made any move to kill her. She felt kind of warm toward him for that. He had all the power.

Bobbi must have blacked out off and on, because slowly she realized that the room was becoming lighter. She saw blood on the bed and felt cold. She didn't connect it all with her head wounds at this time. All she knew was that she was in such pain that she wanted to get away from her head. It hurt so bad that the sex was incidental. Her head seemed huge, and then she realized that the blood was hers. Fear gripped her chest, and she wanted to run. Glancing to the right, she noticed a knife lying next to her head, the man was still on top of her. She stared at the knife, comprehending that there was nothing to stop her from reaching up and stabbing this guy in the back. She weighed the risk for what seemed like an eternity. And it all came down to the fact that she just couldn't do it. The risk of him taking it away and using it on her was too great. Besides, she'd never stabbed another human being before. So she decided to take her chances with him being afraid of being caught in the light.

As it got lighter in the room, Bobbi began to experience some hope, to feel as though she might have a chance. She had been pretending that she was unconscious through most of the attack, so that every time he moved her, she seemed totally limp and lifeless. Suddenly he got up. She heard him buckle his pants. Her hope was replaced by the fear that he might kill her before he left. She was flat on her face now, with a pillow over her head. She couldn't see a thing. It was all black, and she felt something going around her legs. He had taken the clock off the wall and was tying the cord around her feet. He took a piece of clothing and tied her hands behind her back. Then he ran out the patio door.

For a long time Bobbi didn't move. She was afraid to trust the fact that he was gone. She was afraid that he might have sneaked back into the room to see if she was really still alive. Realizing that she was badly hurt, she did finally free herself. She put on a robe and brushed her teeth. It seemed as if her teeth were the only part of her body that she could bear to touch. The rest of her body had somehow been taken away from her, had been somehow hurt. Anger gripped her as she thought about how she had let him live. She felt like a coward. She despised that half of herself that had not allowed her to kill him.

The result of her rape was that Bobbi lost every belief in the concept of a God who was around to take care of people who were good. She lost her sense of security in the world. She felt that she would never be safe anywhere ever again. She lost trust in herself and her body. And with that, she sensed a loss of control over her life. Along with the losses were feelings of numbness and unreality. She questioned how this could have happened to her. Everything in her life was changed, every single thing. She was afraid to sleep at night. She couldn't trust the world around her enough to let go and surrender to slumber. She gave up her apartment, with no place to go. She stopped going to school. Concentration was impossible. She sent her daughter to stay at her brother's house because she couldn't care for herself, much less anyone else. Friends turned away from her because they did not know how to cope with her anger. Relatives were so caught up in their own emotional reactions to her attack that they were not there for her. Bobbi lost her supports; enraged, confused, deeply wounded, she was frightened, and she was all alone.

Network losses burden us with a number of losses all at the same time. They arouse diverse and conflicting feelings, as we saw in Bobbi's case. Loss can present itself in our lives with many faces. Like thunder, it can resonate in the distance or shake us, more directly, to the core of our beings.

## THUNDER AND LOSS AS CHAOTIC

Thunder and loss are both chaotic. Thunder rattles the calm of a lazy, quiet afternoon. It colors the bright sunny day with a dark cloud of gloom. If you've ever been caught in a thunderstorm while picnicking, you understand what I mean. Just think back to the last time that you were in this predicament. You were enjoying the feeling of being outdoors, lying on a blanket in the cool shade, feeling the breeze pass through the trees, while remnants of your picnic lunch sat covered on the wooden table. And then suddenly, the thunder rumbled in. You jumped to your feet, startled, as you began collecting the food, the blanket, and the kids, hurrying as the first drops of rain splattered on you. Within that brief span of time, your peace was interrupted, and your quiet relaxation came to an abrupt end as you scurried about to get out of the rain.

Loss is like that. It too is chaotic. It disrupts our lives. This is its main effect on us. It can cause tremendous upheaval. It throws us off-balance, and this sense of disequilibrium can feel like a threat to our very survival. This threat to our survival comes from the feelings that loss can arouse. It feels like a wound deep inside, a wound from which we may not recover. Some losses feel so great that we feel as if they cannot be endured. The hurt is so deep, the pain is so intense, so overwhelming. We may never have experienced such chaos before. Loss causes our inner world to become shattered, devastated, empty; we feel helpless, confused, and frightened. The intensity of this makes us feel as if we are going to collapse inside, as if we are going to die, as if we are not going to survive this. This disruption propels us back to another time in our lives when we felt this way—back to the time when we were children; uncertain, scared of the monsters that hid under our beds.

Thunder and loss are chaotic. Thunder creates havoc on a calm afternoon. Loss shatters our peace and contentment and throws our lives into chaos.

## THUNDER AND LOSS AS WARNINGS

The way most of us react to loss is to try to repair our disrupted lives. It seems as though our very survival is at stake. How do we accomplish this "rebuilding"? It is through *grief* that we move from the disruption and disequilibrium caused by loss, back to a place of balance and a sense of wholeness. We put our shattered world back together, we mend our wounds, by moving through grief. So our natural reaction to loss is to grieve. Thunder and loss are warnings. Thunder warns of the approaching storm. Loss is the thunder of the approaching storm of grief.

Thunder and loss are similar. They both jar us, steal from us, and scare us. Both wear different faces, are chaotic, and bring warnings. Thunder and loss are both a part of nature, a part of the cycle of all life. We accept thunder in this way, but not loss. How can we allow loss to be part of that same cycle?

Earlier I spoke of a formula for helping us learn to live with loss—a formula that consists of four basic ingredients. By putting the ingredients of this formula to work in our lives, we will be able to begin to accept loss as a natural part of our lives. Let's explore the first ingredient of that formula: permission.

## PERMISSION

Once loss has interrupted our lives, the first thing we need to do is to give ourselves permission—permission to react naturally to our loss, permission to grieve.

What does this mean? Giving ourselves permission to grieve means letting ourselves give in to the feelings of loss. It means letting go of the mask of composure that we usually wear to hide our feelings from ourselves and others. Giving ourselves permission to grieve means allowing ourselves to feel, to hurt, to be confused, to be empty—to just be *where we are in each moment*. Giving ourselves permission to grieve means accepting and embracing our feelings as a valuable part of us, a part which, in time, will help us to heal. Giving ourselves permission to grieve means listening to the gentle voice inside that whispers the way to heal, rather than listening to the people around us who are telling us in subtle ways, or not-so-subtle ways, to be strong, to stop feeling, to stop crying. Giving ourselves permission to grieve means giving ourselves over to the feeling of grief, rather than running from it, hiding from it. Giving ourselves permission to grieve is about opening the inner channel to our inner self.

In my own life, I had been walking around closed off to the feelings of my losses. I was locked up tight inside because I didn't know how to give myself permission to grieve. Then came the loss that really began to crack the armor that I'd always used to hold my feelings in captivity.

*The summer of 1975—I'll be starting the second half of my junior year in college in September. Meanwhile, I'm beginning this job as a summer intern with the state as a counselor aide. I'm working with the Department of Rehabilitation. One of my clients is Delores, a bright, bubbly, twenty-two-year-old woman. She has a congenital hip problem and has had to endure seventeen surgeries over the years. She walks with a limp but doesn't have to use a cane or crutches. She's come in to find a job. The counselor who is supervising me knows her mother and is taking a special interest. He's given Delores a typewriter and dictaphone machine to take home so that she can practice and improve her skills. She's had one job as a secretary that gave her six months of experience. The counselor has been coming down pretty hard on her. In the sensitivity department, he leaves a lot to be desired. He is wanting her to do what he thinks is best for her and is not listening to what she wants for herself. Being somewhat of a fighter, she's given him an ultimatum. If he continues to treat her this way, then she'll just go to an employment agency to look for a job. Sensing her determination, he hands Delores over to me. I've been given instructions to go through the job-bank information each morning, locate appropriate referrals, and pass them along to her. Then I'm to check up on her to make sure that she's going out on them. I'm resentful over the fact that I'm supposed to act like a policeman. As we talk each day, we're getting to know each other. I like Delores. She's warm and open. She's shared with me the loss of her father earlier this year, and how much she misses him. She had received a lot of support and encouragement from him. Feeling as if she is being controlled by the counselor, we decide that she will just deal with me. I will act as an intermediary.*

*I sense that Delores isn't going out on each job referral that I give her, but I'm keeping that to myself because I know the frustration of looking for a job. the pain of rejection when you get turned down. I know how the experience just chips away at your self-confidence, giving you occasional feelings of paralysis. We've been working and getting to know each other for six weeks. Today word came that Delores has gotten a temporary full-time position with the state. The salary is decent, and although it is only a six-month placement, it is experience and a foot in the door. I'm ecstatic. I feel so proud of her and so full of satisfaction. Today, she just glowed.*

*A few weeks have passed and my summer job is about to end. Shortly I'll be back in school making the transition from the working world back into*

*Academia. Delores and I have met for lunch. She seems fairly happy. She says it's difficult for her at work because she is new and has no friends. She's talking about being lonely—how she's been lonely for many years. She's joined the Jehovah's Witnesses, but is quick to assure me that it is not because she is into religion, but because she hopes to meet a man. She says she's never had a date and that surprises me. She's a very attractive woman. She says that throughout her years in school the boys stayed away from her because they didn't want to be seen with a cripple. What she wants most right now is to have a boyfriend. Joining the Jehovah's Witnesses is her way of attaining this. She feels accepted there. We're talking about meeting again for lunch in a few weeks, once I get settled back into the school routine.*

*I ought to call Delores and set up our lunch date. No, I'd better wait a few days. I've got this paper to write. Christmas time already, and still I haven't called Delores. I wonder how she's doing? Four finals coming up next week. I'll reach her later. Where has the time gone? Valentine's Day and Rudy and I are down here on the mall looking for a card. Somebody is calling my name. I know that voice. The counselor I worked for at Rehab is motioning for me to come over. We're busy exchanging niceties. "Huh? Oh yeah, I remember Delores. How is she doing?" "Early in January she took an overdose of pills and died," he replies. My knees are weakening, my legs are shaking and unsure, my stomach feels like it has just sustained a blow. Words crowd into my mind. Why? How? No! I'm too stunned to speak. The counselor's voice is breaking through my thoughts and reaching my ears. "Well, it's really all for the better. At least she's out of her misery now." I'm standing here in disbelief that Delores' life and death are being so casually dismissed. Every cell in my body is rearing back in opposition. The words I want to shout stay lodged in my throat: "You rotten son-of-a-bitch! You cold-hearted creep! How dare you!" I'm immobilized, frozen, saying nothing as he describes how Delores had fallen down the stairs a few days prior to her death and how she had been in a lot of pain since the fall. How she had overdosed on pain pills. Now he's mouthing something about how hard her mother is taking it and is crediting himself with how well he's helping her to deal with it. I'm rooted here to the sidewalk, caught between trying to grasp the reality that Delores is dead by her own hand, and a fantasy of stomping that insensitive jerk on his ever-so-objective face. I'm walking in a daze. I can't even cry.*

This time my armory of defenses against allowing a loss to be fully experienced was badly shaken. My guilt was heavy. Maybe if I had taken the time to call her as I'd promised, it would have made a difference. I couldn't escape the guilt that was gnawing at me. This loss was different than all the others because it could have been prevented. Slowly, I began to allow myself to feel, to feel the confusion and the guilt. Since I was feeling a small piece of this loss, the guilt, I had to do something with it. I wouldn't allow myself to lock this away, so I took another baby step toward giving myself permission to grieve in my own unique way. I became a crisis counselor at the local suicide prevention center in an attempt to understand why a person takes his or her own life.

What I came to understand was a lot about myself. Delores' death had cracked the protective shell that had housed all my feelings about all my losses. As my armor began to weaken, the illusion of my immunity to loss also weakened, and my inner world was in conflict. As a crisis counselor, I was in a situation in which I had to come face to face with loss through death, and this was my way of beginning to give myself permission to grieve. I learned that feelings are valuable and that they are valid. I found that no one can hide from feelings of loss. They don't just go away. They are carried around inside until they are "owned" and expressed. My illusion of immunity to the feelings of loss was completely and permanently shattered in the call that I shared with a woman dying from the disabling disease—the call that made me come to grips with the possibility that I too might have a serious illness, and that I too might have to deal with my feelings surrounding that loss. It all began to come together.

*I'm at a turning point in my life. All this running and hiding is overwhelming me. I feel so heavy, so burdened. I can't carry it all by myself any longer. I feel dead inside. This is so painful. If I have M.S., I'm going to die. I don't want to die feeling this bad. I've got nothing to lose now. If I get into these feelings, if I lose control, if I go crazy, I've got nothing to lose because I might die anyway. If I don't do something I'll go crazy for sure. God, I'm scared. There's no place to hide any more. At the psychodrama workshop I've been going to I've seen lots of people let go of control—go crazy for a while—and every one of them has come out on the other side of it feeling renewed and whole. If they can do it, why can't I? I have to do it. I have no choice. Doing nothing, denying, running, hiding isn't working anymore. I'm so afraid of my feelings.*

*Here I am. Tonight is the night. I've brought Rudy, Cindy, and Dick along for moral support. I need their strength and caring. I wish they could do it for me. God, I'm so scared. My mouth is so dry that I can barely get words out. There's Robert. He's the facilitator. I need to trust him. I have to hand my controls over to him. I will. He cares. That's what counts. I have to trust myself. I have to care enough about myself to trust me. No way to chicken out now. I'm out here in the center of a group of thirty people, requesting that I work first. That's so I won't have a chance to run out the door. I can't believe that I'm doing this, baring my soul. Bring on the demons, there's no turning back now. "I don't want to die," wails the woman who is on the floor. Who is making those awful, angry sounds? It's me! I never knew I could sound like this. Robert encourages me to stay with it. I trust him. I sense his gentleness and caring.*

*My first confrontation is with the demon of multiple sclerosis. I'm in an altered state of consciousness right now, staring into the face of my fears about the disease. I'm visualizing having the disease. This is real, as my body cripples itself while I wrestle with the monster—the loss of control of*

*my legs, arms, and speech. Now I've lost my sight and I'm totally depend-*
*ent, helpless, a vegetable. The fears seem to lose their powerful grip on me*
*as I experience them in face-to-face combat. I've uncovered another*
*demon—my own death.*

*I take the suggestion, hesitating for a brief moment, to die—to experience*
*my death. It is so dark and cold. I have no body, I'm floating. "What is the*
*worst part of dying?" questions Robert. "Leaving all the people who are*
*close to me—having to say goodbye," I reply automatically. Now I'm say-*
*ing goodbye to all the people I value. My heart is breaking. I'm really here.*
*I'm sobbing, feeling incredible pain that I didn't know existed. Years of*
*forgotten tears are rising up through my body and spilling out, as I hold,*
*touch, and finish with each significant person in my life. I've lost all con-*
*cept of time. The now moment of saying goodbye is all that exists. This*
*now moment seems to last forever. There are so many people I love, so*
*much to say to each of them, so very many tears.*

*It's over now as I lie down again and re-experience my death. "What is*
*the worst part of being dead?" asks Robert gently. "Being so very alone,"*
*I respond. "At what other time in your life have you felt this alone?"*
*guides Robert. The corner of the kitchen, the coolness of the green wall,*
*me seated on the beer case, shaking, crying—the image flashes through my*
*consciousness. The insight dawns, illuminating my awareness. I've come*
*full-circle. Everything is so clear to me now. Facing the demons about M.S.,*
*my death, my grief at having to say goodbye, are only the beginning. My*
*path is set in front of me. My journey encompasses exploring, accepting,*
*and expressing the myriad of feelings surrounding all of my losses. I'm*
*feeling freed up. I'm feeling light. I'm feeling incredibly alive and excited*
*as I embrace my path. Now that I know the way I am no longer frightened,*
*because my path with its heaviness, work, and pain leads to a richer, fuller*
*life and personal insight and growth. It's all about movement. It's all about*
*being alive!*

Finally, I had given myself the permission to grieve. I stopped running and
hiding when I let myself go into the feelings, through the psychodrama. I took
off my mask of composure and allowed my feelings their free expression. I literally "lost face." They were okay wherever they took me. Within the expression of these feelings, I allowed the inner channel to open.

Permission to grieve also came to me in three others ways: through awareness, contact, and validation.

Awareness of the state I was in motivated me to seek out the help I
needed. I was so locked up within that I couldn't do it alone. I was vaguely
aware that something was really wrong in my life, that I was half, not whole. I
knew I had to confront my own death in order to live. That was coming from
the inner voice deep inside. The awareness helped to give me courage to give
myself the permission to delve into my feelings of grief.

Being in contact with a community of caring people who were willing to support me and guide me through this frightening new territory of feelings made it easier to grant myself permission. Seeing that others had gone through it and had survived helped, too.

The validation of my feelings—being with people who did not judge, who did not try to shut down my feelings, but who instead accepted me, accepted my feelings—this helped me to accept them, too. The validation by others that my feelings were okay encouraged me to permit myself to express them. So all these things helped me to learn that I was *allowed* to grieve.

## HOW YOU MIGHT CREATE PERMISSION

Permission to grieve has to come from you and to you. First, there has to be an opening that comes from within. The following exercise is a way to begin to allow yourself the permission to explore the feeling of grief.

Opening the Channel. Take some time now to stop the world outside. Begin to turn your attention inward. Assume a position of comfort, uncrossing your arms and legs. Close your eyes for a few minutes and allow yourself to relax. Take a sheet of paper and begin to explore your feelings by answering the following questions. Do not censor any thought, word, or image that comes to you. Simply record whatever presents itself to you. Allow any feelings that bubble up. If tears come, allow their flow. If anger comes, let it be okay.

Picture your life space as a whole circle—continuous and unified. Now think back and remember three times in your life when pieces of that circle were cut out—three times when you lost a valued person, place, object, role, or part of yourself. List these three major losses on a piece of paper.

Choose that loss which has the most emotional meaning for you now.

Reflect on that time in your life—see it as if it were a movie flashing by on the screen of your mind's eye.

List some of the feelings you had at the time of this loss.

Ask yourself, *Where in my body do I still hold some of these feelings?*
Go there.

What does the grief feel like here? (Allow a picture or thought to come.) What form does it take? What color is is? What is its texture?

Begin a dialogue with your feelings—ask: *What feeling are you? Are you rage, anger, hurt, guilt?* Allow it to come to you in its own time.

*You live here in my body. How do you show yourself* (through headaches, nausea, diarrhea, backaches)?

*Why are you here? What is your function?*
*Do I still need you for any reason?*
*What do I have to do to begin to let you go?*
Now that the channel is open, is there any message for you to carry away?
Ask yourself, *Have I permission to feel you and let you go?*

This exercise is a way for allowing permission to come from you. Permission can also come to you.

Awareness, contact, and validation are all tied to creating permission. In Chapter Two, "The Storm," I hope to give you these three components.

Learning about grief—what it is, its process—will give you an added bit of awareness. Knowing about grief lessens the fear of it, and ridding yourself of fear will make it easier to give yourself permission.

Seeing how others have dealt with grief, and the ways in which they moved through the process, will provide support and contact.

Understanding that what you are feeling is not only normal and natural, but it is healing; it will validate your experience of grief. Seeing that others do strange things while they are grieving will validate your own belief that you are not the only one who is experiencing bizarre thoughts, feelings, and behaviors, that you are not crazy, that you are merely healing.

Exercises, designed to help you develop skills for grieving as you move through its various phases, will also be presented, along with the second ingredient in the formula for living with loss: Creating an atmosphere of trust.

chapter two

# THE STORM

Mary had lived in fear since her husband's heart attack in August 1974. They had been married for thirty-seven years and had raised three children. They had endured together the loss of their first-born to cancer. They had shared the joy of watching their grandchildren grow. Mary depended so much on him. He was her life. Mary was frightened because this attack warned her of what was to come. She couldn't imagine how she could survive if he should die. Their lives were entwined as one life. He took care of everything. He took care of her. When she awakened at 6:30 A.M. on that day in November, a little more than a year after his attack, she knew immediately that something was wrong. He was making a gurgling sound and she could not wake him. By the time help arrived a short while later, he was gone. Mary's worst fear had come true. She had lost her beloved Blas and was left behind, scared and alone. The thunder of this loss brought to her the storm of grief. Mary lived in fear at the thought of her loss because grief, the aftermath, is frightening.

## GRIEF IS SCARY

Grief frightens each and every one of us. It arouses feelings that we may never have felt before. The intensity of these feelings overwhelms us so that our very survival is threatened.

Mary felt the most anguish in the evenings, alone in the house that she and Blas had shared. She missed him terribly and longed to feel his arms around her. It was devastating as she tried to get used to sleeping alone after having slept in his arms for thirty-eight years. Sometimes she felt angry with him for leaving her, as though he had wanted to die. He'd often told her that the worst thing about having to die was having to leave her. Now, seeing couples together often brought twinges of jealousy as she realized again that she was now half of what used to be a whole. This wrenched her apart inside.

Grief is scary because everything is different. Our whole life changes. And the slow realization that it is never going to be the same, ever again, robs us of familiarity, of the known in our lives.

Many times Mary would see his parked car in front and would go to the door expecting him to be coming up the walk. And then she'd remember, and the cold, harsh reality of her loss pushed in on her. Being a very private person, Mary had shared her innermost thoughts and feelings only with Blas. For a long time after his death, she would think, "Oh, I must tell Blas," and then she'd remember that she could never tell him anything—ever again. Something on TV would bring back a memory of her life with Blas, and she'd be reminded again that it would be no more. And the rain would fall. She'd find herself sobbing.

Grief is scary because our life lies in front of us, shattered. Who we were and what we were no longer exist. We are frightened because we are faced with a vast unknown. There we stand, asking ourselves, "what happens now? What am I supposed to do?" Much of the fear of grief comes from being shattered by our loss and not knowing what to do with all the pieces. The human reaction to loss is to grieve. Understanding and learning more about the human condition of grief makes it less frightening.

## LESSENING OUR FEAR

Three ways to lessen our fear about grief are to look at what it is, to examine what we know about it, and to begin to see it in a different light.

### What is Grief?

Grief is like a storm. As a storm moves in with its howling, raging winds and torrential rains, it seems as though nature is mourning. The world appears to change. It puts on a face of gloom, as the grey overcast skies cast a shadow of darkness. During the storm we are forced to retreat indoors until the storm is over. The normal pace of the world outside winds down to a standstill as the storm rages on. Yet even as the storm roars, a mood of quiet reflection is created as the raindrops, falling steadily on the rooftops, tap out a hypnotic cadence.

Grief also moves in with howling anguish and torrents of sobbing rain as we begin to experience our loss. Our lives change. A sense of greyness clouds our perception of the world. The storm of grief forces us to retreat inward, to confront and feel the intense emotions aroused by our loss. The storm of grief creates devastating thoughts, feelings, and experiences. This picture of grief is particularly true of a loss due to death. It dramatically shows the anguish, anger, and pain that are part of the storm. All types of loss carry these feelings. The intensity depends upon how much of ourself we invest in our loss.

No one can exist today without experiencing grief in a thousand ways. In a society that changes as rapidly as ours due to increased technology, the opportunities for loss are especially commonplace. As progress and growth accelerate, change occurs constantly, and sometimes abruptly. Those of us living in twentieth-century America are presented with the enormous task of integrating the losses that come as a part of change. All painful losses must be grieved. People today may be in a constant state of grief. So there is a tremendous need to know what grief is and to lessen our fear of it.

Earlier we saw our lives in the symbol of a complete and whole circle. Every person, place, or thing that we value is part of the circle. Loss was seen as an outside event that broke the continuity and unity of our lifespace, leaving a gap or empty spot in our lives. That gap, the result of loss, is gradually filled in by grieving, which eventually restores balance and wholeness.

Grief has been defined by various researchers. Colin Murray Parkes sees grief as a "reaction, emotional and behavioral, which occurs when a love tie is severed."[1] Edgar Jackson expands on the definition of grief, as related to the loss of a loved one:

> It is essentially the emotional and related reactions that occur at the time of and following the loss by death of an important person in the emotional life of an individual who has reached the state of development where he has the capacity for object love. Grief is the emotion that is involved in the work of mourning, whereby a person seeks to disengage himself from the demanding relationship that has existed—and to reinvest his emotional capital in new and producing directions for the health and welfare of his future life in society.[2]

Expanded further, grief can be seen as the reaction to any important loss. It is not limited exclusively to losses experienced through death. If we invest emotional energy into a relationship, an event, a role, a place, an object, image, or symbol, and that is lost, then our reaction to that loss is still to grieve. Ira

Tanner's definition of grief seems more complete: "Grieving is basically mourning the lost parts of ourselves that we invested in a person, place or object that we have lost."[3] So what is grief? It is a mourning of the lost part of ourselves—the time, energy, attention, and feelings that we gave to the person, place, or object we have lost. Through our mourning, we gradually reclaim that part of us that we had given away, so that later we will have it to give away again, in new and different directions.

The words *grief, bereavement,* and *mourning* are used extensively in research literature. Grief is usually applied to describe the general, overall reaction to loss. Bereavement and mourning normally denote the type of grief peculiar to loss through death of a loved one. As we explore this subject, all three words will be used synonymously and interchangeably to refer to the human reaction to all types of loss.

Most of the literature that describes our current knowledge about grief relates it to loss by death. As we examine what is known about grief, keep in mind that these descriptions can be expanded to include reactions to any type of of loss, though the intensity and duration may vary depending on the type of loss and the value of what has been lost to the individual.

Storms bring dark, gloomy skies as the clouds burst with torrents of rain. Grief brings darkness and gloom as our hearts break with showers of tears for what we have lost of ourselves.

## What Do We Know About Grief?

It has just been in recent years that social scientists have taken up the task of investigating what people go through as they mourn. In *The First Year of Bereavement,* Glick, Weiss, and Parkes provide a summary of the research on grief.[4] Thomas Elliot (1932), an American sociologist, was one of the first researchers to attempt to develop an accurate description of grief and a theory that would offer some explanation of it. Emphasizing the importance of bereavement as a time of crisis, Elliot characterized some of the initial impact of the grief experience:

> He noted that among the immediate impacts of bereavement are a sense of abandonment, shock and denial, colored by guilt and sometimes anger, and accompanied by intense and persistent longing for the one who has died. In addition, he spoke of the disruption of accustomed patterns that bereavement produced.[5]

An extention of Elliot's work on typical reactions to bereavement was conducted by D. M. Fulcomer (1942) in systematic interviews with 72 bereaved men and women. The conclusion of this investigation was that the healing process consists of five phases beginning with a sense of shock and ending with "a stage of 'repatterning' in which the individual has established a new and stable way of life."[6]

In his paper "Mourning and Melancholia," Freud (1914) saw grief as the means by which the libidinal energy that connects the individual to the loved object is gradually withdrawn:

> This energy was conceived by Freud as being bound to the memories and ideas that arose from interactions with the dead person. To become free of his tie to this person, the energy has to be detached by a process Freud termed "hypercathexis," a process that requires the mourner to turn his back on the real world, and to invest free energy in the struggle to 'decathect' the loved object. By focusing his mind on the lost person and bringing to consciousness each relevant memory, the mourner gradually sets free the bound energy.[7]

Since Freud's explanation proved to be rather abstract, leaving many unanswered questions about the dynamics of grief, a number of present-day researchers have developed alternative models to explain the reaction to loss. John Bowlby (1969) proposed a theory that emphasized prior experience, biochemical and neurophysiological changes, and the attachment to a significant other as determinants of the individual's perceptions and behavior in the area of grieving. Separation from valued people, in Bowlby's theory, was likely to trigger behavior patterns that represented attempts to get the loved one back. This contradicts Freud's position that grief is a way of disengaging one's self from the lost loved one; ". . . Bowlby's theory implies that far from promoting separation, grief has the biological function of promoting reunion."[8]

In 1972, Colin Murray Parkes concluded that "grief is a process of realization, of making real inside the self an event that has already occurred in the reality outside."[9]

The pioneering efforts of Erich Lindemann provide descriptions of the consequences of totally unexpected traumatic loss. He accepts Freud's concepts, but expands upon them and produces additional details. In his paper "The Symptomology and Management of Acute Grief,"[10] attention is drawn to grief as a definite syndrome with specific psychological and body symptoms. Lindemann observed 101 people who had suffered a loss: people labeled as psychoneurotics who had lost a relative during the course of treatment; relatives of patients who had died in the hospital; relatives of members of the armed forces; and bereaved survivors of the 1942 Coconut Grove fire.

The symptoms of acute grief that he noted were bodily distress, a preoccupation with the image of the lost loved one, guilt and anger reactions, and a loss of normal patterns of behavior.

### Bodily Distress

The most common features symbolizing distress in the body were a tendency to sigh, a sense of a loss of strength, feelings of being drained and exhausted, feelings of emptiness in the pit of the stomach, dryness in the mouth, and no desire to eat.

### Preoccupation with the Image of the Lost Loved One

This preoccupation showed itself in three ways: auditory hallucinations in which the person experienced hearing the voice of the lost one call out; hypnagogic hallucinations, in which the grieving person saw, as if in a vision, the lost one; and the experience of catching glimpses of the deceased—for instance, on the street, getting on a bus, or in a crowd.

### Guilt Reaction

The guilt reaction was characterized with derisive feelings of self-accusation and self-reproach for not doing the "right" things for the lost one.

### Anger Reaction

The anger reaction is characterized by loss of sensitivity and connection in relationships with friends and family members, along with feelings of irritability and isolation.

### Loss of Normal Patterns of Behavior

Changes in patterns of usual behavior that people reported were restlessness, hyperactivity without a way to channel the energy, an inability to begin and maintain normal daily behavior. A loss of social skills was also evident.

Lindemann also noticed that genuine grief reactions were found in persons who experienced bereavement due to the loss of a person through separation rather than through death. These grief reactions were seen in the group he studied in which a member of the family had gone into the armed forces, so Lindemann concluded that grief is not exclusive to loss through death. "Acute bereavement from any cause, be it death, disillusionment, separation, or loss through geographical removal, brings in its train a well marked symptom complex . . ."[11]

As people began to tell what grief was like and as researchers began to listen, the phenomenon of grief began to emerge as being much more than a brief emotional response to loss. It became apparent that rather than being a temporary time of sadness or a disease state, grief is a *process*. The notion of grief as a process allows us to understand it as more than merely a brief time of sadness that begins and ends abruptly. A process indicates that grief takes time and that people move through different phases in their reaction to loss.

So what do we know about grief? We know that bereavement is a time of crisis that brings with it intense, overwhelming feelings. We know that grief is the way in which loss becomes real for us, and that it involves psychological and physical symptoms. We know that we grieve over all types of loss, that grief is not exclusive to loss by death. We know that grief is not a temporary state that is soon over. It is a process. Let's examine grief in that light. Understanding grief in this way will lessen our fear.

## Seeing Grief in a Different Light

Rather than seeing grief as a monster from which we must run and hide, we need to look at it in terms of its being a process—a process of healing. What is "process"? Process is a journey of unfolding, of becoming. Just as the caterpillar passes through different phases on its way to becoming a butterfly, we too must pass through several stages as we grieve. A process is a journey that takes us through an experience, in and out of different doors, down different hallways, until we come out the other end. Grief is like that. We have to go through it to come out on the other side of it. We can't dance around it. We can't step over it. We can't back away from it. We have to go *through* it. Unfolding takes time. In order to unfold we pass through varying phases. A storm is an example of an unfolding, evolving process. It moves through different phases. At first we hear the thunder in the distance. As the storm moves closer, louder claps of thunder are followed by bolts of lightning lighting up the sky. With the storm comes the rain. And after the rainfall, the sun peeks through the few remaining clouds and again brightens the day. The storm is a process.

In grieving there is a process. There is unfolding, becoming. We move from the initial devastation—from being wounded, empty, and disrupted by the loss—to becoming full, whole, and in balance once again. Healing takes time. So grieving is a slow healing process, a journey that leads from loss, devastation, and disruption to growth, gain, and harmony. Loss leaves an empty space in the circle of our lives. Grief is the process that allows us to fill in the gap.

John Bowlby described the process of mourning as consisting of three phases: (1) denial and shock, (2) disorganization, and (3) reorganization.[12] Colin Murray Parkes, from his work with widows in London during their first year of bereavement, proposed a model of grief as a process that brings all the previous research into sharp focus.[13] This model consists of four stages: numbness/shock, searching/pining, depression, and restructuring. The model will be used as the basis for the discussion of passing through the process of grief in this book. We will examine the stages in detail a little later.

It is important to keep in mind that the study of grief is still in the pioneering stages. The process we will be exploring is a model. It is a general description of the unfolding journey that bereaved people have experienced. There is no "true" or "right" or "correct way" to grieve. We have no definitive answers because the information on this subject is scarce. The grief process we describe is a model; it provides an anchor for us to cling to as we pass through the turbulence of grief. Knowing about the process of grief gives us an idea of what grief feels like. It can provide us with an understanding of our experience and behavior as we pass through grief. Each of us has a unique journey through grief. Since we are all different, we grieve differently. We will probably relate to some of the experiences of this process, but maybe not all of it. The important thing to remember is to go with your own unique process as you grieve. If it differs from this model, do not fall into judging yourself, or worrying that your experience with grief is "wrong" because it is not the same. This model is used to give us some understanding of our experience in the reaction to loss. Reality is our individual experience, and flowing with that is what is important. Sift through what this model has to offer and take that in, then cast aside what doesn't fit for you.

In the following two chapters, we will be looking closely at each stage of Parkes' model of the grief process. We will examine what each stage is about, what it feels like, and how to get through it. We will first be concerned with the first two stages, numbness/shock and searching/pining. Then, we will concentrate on the stages of depression and restructuring. Finally, we will examine how grief becomes scary, and look at how not to buy into this fear.

# chapter three

# THE MIRE

Blue, then white, then blue, then white, linoleum tiles taking diamond shapes or square shapes depending on how you look at them. Mary turned the gas on under the coffee pot. Blue and yellow flames danced up the side. The kitchen looked so much smaller than when I was a kid. Blas has been gone for one year. Mary is my aunt. I sipped coffee out of the green porcelain cup with its chipped handle and listened as she talked about how it had been for her after he died. She said that there comes a point when you're all alone with it. A point where you have to either sink or swim. She remembered aloud the moments of wishing she were with him, wishing she could join him in death. Confusion, pain, isolation, the aloneness of it all shadowed her face.

## How Do We Grieve?

Grieving seems to consist of an unfolding process as we evolve from the disruption and injury of loss to being healed and whole once again. We will now examine the paths that grief seems to take. As we watch the way in which the process moves, we will also see how three different people with three different types of loss passed through the storm of grief. We met them earlier—Louise, who with her husband Dewey lost a five-year-old daughter through death; Bill, who lost an important aspect of himself, his health; and Bobbi, who suffered a network of losses as a result of being brutally raped. We will see how each of them dealt with their loss as they moved through their own processes of grief.

Grieving, according to Colin Murray Parkes, has four stages: numbness/shock, searching/pining, depression, and restructuring. Let us look at the first two stages. We'll explore what each stage is about, what each stage feels like, and some ways to get through each phase.

## NUMBNESS/SHOCK

### What Is It About?

The day Jenny died was all kind of a jumble for Louise. Jenny had lapsed into a coma at home and Louise, sensing that something had happened, rushed her to the hospital. It seemed that as soon as they got there she had stopped breathing. The next thing Louise knew, one of the doctors was gently guiding her into a room and closing the door. It was like a dream from which she couldn't wake up. She was in shock. Louise had just one thought that kept going through her mind: "What am I going to do now?" She moved from the hospital to home as if she were floating. She had known it was coming. She'd known all along that Jenny was dying from leukemia, and yet now, as it was happening, as she lost her, Louise simply could not believe it.

This initial stage of grief is typically characterized by numbness, alarm, or shock, and begins immediately upon experiencing the loss. Shock tends to serve as a cushion, numbing us for a little while to the full impact of the loss. It gives us some time before we completely begin to absorb the fact or the reality of the loss. This period of numbness gives us a brief rest from feeling. We feel nothing, and everything around us takes on an unreal quality. Louise could not believe that it had happened. For her, none of it was real. She could not believe that she had lost Jenny. During shock, we know about the loss in our head, but in our gut it is still unknown. We feel split. We know and yet we don't know. We act and yet we feel nothing. It's as though we are on automatic; we go through the motions, we attend to what needs to be done—and yet at the same time, we feel detached, separate from it, all because we can't grasp it. It just isn't real.

### What Does It Feel Like?

Shock seems to take on the form of various physical and psychological disturbances.

*Physical Disturbances*

Some of the symptoms that people report feeling in their bodies during this time are numbness, a loss of appetite, emptiness in the pit of the stomach, sighing, headaches, insomnia, muscular aches, lethargy, and decreased strength and stamina. The somatic symptoms that Lindemann noted (see page 41) are incorporated into this phase. These physical reactions leave us feeling as though we can no longer function.

After the rape, Bobbi stopped sleeping at night. It was as though she had to stay awake, on guard, to protect herself. She felt numb. Food was no longer of any concern to her. She didn't feel like eating. The thought of food made her gag. There was no way that food could fill the emptiness within. Exhaustion and weakness seemed to be her constant companions. She couldn't walk from one room to another without having to lie down. There was no recognition or awareness of her body. For a long time she felt as though she were walking around inside a hollow shell. Bobbi saw herself as a wounded animal, retreating back into the shadows.

For Bobbi, this first stage of grief brought on intense disturbances in her body. She experienced insomnia and loss of appetite, as well as being drained of her normal strength and stamina. Her shock left her with a physical sense of emptiness.

*Psychological Disturbances*

Losing Jennifer was the hardest thing that Louise had ever been through. Having Jenny was living one day at a time, enjoying her, marveling that she was alive and at the strides she was making. Losing her left a big, empty feeling, a vacuum. Louise missed the very presence of her lovely child. She was gone, never to be seen again. Louise felt it in her heart mostly, where her love had been. It was a big, empty hole. Louise was anxious and restless now, getting up in the morning, always finding something else to clean in the house. At times she seemed to be climbing the walls. She had excessive energy, so she painted the living room and the dining room and hall. Then she painted the bedroom and moved all of Jenny's things out of there. She found herself in perpetual motion. She planted flowers and dug up weeds. She liked ripping away at the weeds because they didn't talk back. She did a lot of sewing and took classes. There was a need to fill the time, the time that had been devoted to Jenny for so many years. She needed desperately to fill up this space with activity. Her mind was fuzzy, dazed. She told her husband, Dewey, that her brain felt like Jell-O. Re-entry back into the world was not coming easily. It was as though she were on the outside of things looking in.

The psychological disturbances experienced during this phase of grief are restless anxiety, emptiness, worry, confusion, hyperactivity, and irritability. Earlier we saw that the physical symptoms of this stage included lethargy and decreased strength and stamina. Both lethargy and excessive energy are apt to be in this stage. How can this be? These diverse disturbances are episodic. At times during this phase the bereaved person feels drained and lethargic. At other times there is excessive energy with an inability to channel that energy into an organized activity. The grieving person seems to be in a state of high arousal during much of this initial stage. At times the intensity of it brings on a sort of panic. Louise experienced this sense of hyperactivity with a need to fill each waking moment. This state of high arousal had Louise feeling as though she were out of control. She saw her behavior as strange and bizarre.

Irritability plagued Bill when he learned about the loss of his health. Knowing that he now had to live with a disease, he felt betrayed, as if someone or something had taken away his health. He was short-tempered with people, snapping at friends, relatives, and doctors. He found himself taking it out on them, as if it was somehow their fault. He felt unable to control this irritability. He also saw his behavior as strange.

In actuality, neither Louise's nor Bill's behavior is strange. Their behaviors are typical of someone who is in shock from the impact of loss. It is as though, psychologically, we know that the time isn't right yet to begin to feel our loss, so we must keep busy. Irritability is a cover for the feelings just below the surface that are getting ready to break through. These psychological disturbances may be our way of clearing a space for ourselves, keeping the feelings at bay because we are not yet ready, or able, to deal with them.

The numbness/shock stage of grief feels unreal. That's because the feelings of loss are not yet real. We are in an emotional and physical shock where we just stop. We freeze. We shut everything down temporarily. We are unable to feel the loss just yet so we keep a lid on it. The restless anxiety, hyperactivity, worry, confusion, and irritability are what leak out. We use them to keep us from feeling. At this point the feelings of loss are too intense, too overwhelming. It is during this stage that we give ourselves some space so that we can allow it in, a little at a time.

## Some Ways to Get Through This Stage

The shock that we experience from a loss gives a severe blow to our bodies and emotions. We are injured, deeply hurt. When an animal is wounded it goes off and finds a place that is safe. There it rests, eating little, taking in liquid nourishment. It begins to nurture itself as a part of the process of healing. So it is, too, with human beings. We are hurt by any kind of traumatic loss. Our initial reaction to the loss is a sense of deep shock. Shock is a time out. It is time away from knowing the reality of the loss. Like an injured animal, we need to find a haven, a safe place where we can pull back and rest, a place where we can begin to take care—of our bodies and our emotions, as part of the healing process. We need to begin to take care by tuning in to ourselves, by sensing our needs at this time. We need to take tender care of ourselves—our bodies and feelings—before we are ready to face the reality of our loss. There are some ways in which we can help ourselves as we pass through shock: we can allow the shock to *be,* we can give our bodies loving care, we can put our minds to rest, and we can take care of our feelings.

### Allowing the Shock to Be

We must go through shock. It is the first step in healing. It is vital to allow the shock or numbness, as uncomfortable as it is, to *be.* We must allow ourselves to be there. So one way of moving through this stage of grief is by permitting ourselves to be where we are. The way to *be* is to ignore and stop harsh judgments on ourselves, or lectures to ourselves for the ways we are feeling or behaving.

We need to be where we are and to allow that to be okay. Our initial reactions to loss are different, since we are all unique individuals. Some of us will be strong and stoic as loss first intrudes upon our lives; we may feel numb, with no tears flowing, going through the motions as we take care of business. Others of us, once we hear of the loss, will be angry, will protest, or scream, or weep and wail. We don't react the same. The important thing is to let ourselves be, however that is for us. If your way is to be strong and stoic, then *be there.* If your way is to yell and cry out in protest, then *be there.* Allow your shock, your unique way of being with it, to simply be, with no judgments, no self-recriminations. Allow it to be, not good or bad, just as it is. We have to go through the shock and come out at the other end so we can move on in our healing. But while we have to allow it, there are some other ways to soften its impact.

### Giving our Bodies Loving Care

The shock that we experience from our loss causes physical and psychological disturbances that sap us of strength and energy. Our bodies are in need of loving care. Since exhaustion and fatigue are a result of shock, rest is a way of replenishing and renewing our bodies from the wound of our loss. Take as much rest as you need during these initial weeks. The need to doze and nap often during the day may be there. Allow that rest for your body. Tune in to the messages that your body is sending you. You are recovering from shock. Rest is needed.

Eating good nutritious food is another way of giving care to our bodies. In the beginning it is often difficult to eat because much of the time our appetite is gone. During this time eat warm, gentle foods such as hot broth. Eat foods that feel healing as they enter your body.

When my sister-in-law left a fourteen-year marriage, the impact of the loss was tremendous. It was as though something had reached deep inside and wrenched everything out of her. She was incredibly weak. Walking up a flight of stairs left her exhausted. For the first few weeks she needed care. The first night she stayed with me I sensed the need to mother her. I gave her warm milk and tucked her into bed. She was hurting and in need of tenderness.

Let the people in your life who care about you know that you need their tenderness. This is a time when we need all the love we can get. Open up to the caring that those around us have to give. Allow it. Drink it in. And ask for it.

Soft exercise such as yoga or t'ai chi help to soothe the physical aches and muscular pains brought on by the impact of loss. Walking among the trees and grass gives needed physical movement. Getting out in the fresh air and making a connection with nature's life process adds some comfort as we begin on our journey through grief.

Pampering ourselves with hot bubble baths, or being touched, as in body massage, are other ways to physically nurture ourselves while we are in the state of numbness.

### Putting Our Minds to Rest

Everything seems magnified at night. When we have the flu, we usually feel more achy, more feverish, more miserable once the sun has gone down. In shock, we may find that we can't sleep. Everything about our loss seems bigger. It all seems distorted, out of proportion. We may lie in bed and find our eyes wide open. We may toss and turn, unable to get comfortable, unable to relax, unable to turn off the thoughts that are racing through our minds. Insomnia is usually tied to the mind being wide awake, speeding, chattering, loudly playing thoughts and scenarios that keep our bodies taut and restless. Sleep is kept away. With insomnia it's important to get up and "put our heads to bed." We need to put our minds to sleep so that the rest of us can fall into slumber. One way of lulling the mind is to get a pencil and paper and begin jotting down the thoughts in your head. Don't analyze, don't judge, don't censor—merely record. Once the thoughts are put down on paper, they are no longer being carried around in our heads, causing a noisy babble. Talking into a tape recorder is another means for getting busy thoughts out of our heads. Once we free the thoughts by letting them out, we lighten up inside and quiet down. We need to release the heaviness and become light.

Another way of quieting our mind and tucking it away for the night is by lullaby. Mothers have known this trick for centuries. Listen to soft, caressing music that soothes and has the effect of hugging. This allows the mind to rest. The rhythmic motion of a rocking chair also can bring soothing, gentle rest. A cup of warm milk helps to relax the tight muscles that keep us locked into wakefulness.

And lastly, reading until our eyes begin to grow heavy helps put the mind to sleep.

### Ways of Caring for Our Feelings

Connected to these physical disturbances are the upsets in our psychological life. They are not separate, the body and the feelings. They intermingle. One affects the other. One acts upon the other. So as we take care of one, this has an effect on the other. As we soothe our physical aches, say through soft exercise, we release the tension that was held in our bodies and in doing this, we reduce anxiety. When we find ways of reducing anxiety and worry, we can feel our tight, tense muscles begin to relax. So we can help ourselves via either channel, the physical or the psychological. When we help ourselves through one channel, we automatically affect the other one.

One way of psychologically easing the impact of the restless anxiety and hyperactivity associated with the sense of shock is to allow ourselves to do whatever activity it is that we need to be doing. We might ask ourselves these questions: "What is it that I need to be doing with all of this restlessness?" "What is it that I need to do to make myself feel better?" "What is it that I need to be doing to take care of myself?" We need to get in touch with our intuition, with that part of ourselves that knows everything, that knows what we need, and let it speak to us. If we let ourselves get into a relaxed state, if we are patient, if we wait without analyzing or judging, if we just *be,* quietly, our answer will come. Once we have a sense of what we need to do, we can do it. For Louise it was painting room after room in her house, and digging weeds, and doing volunteer work, and sewing. She didn't criticize or analyze her actions or judge herself for what she was doing. She just went with it. She just did what she sensed she had to do. So the main thing is to allow ourselves to do whatever it is we need to do without analysis or judgments. We need to follow our own healing process.

We need to allow the feelings of worry and confusion to be and to say them out loud. Give the feeling a voice. If confusion and worry have a voice, then they get sorted out and eventually dissipate. So talk about the thoughts and feelings with people in your life who can listen, and who can hear them.

Acknowledge your feelings of irritability. It is okay to be annoyed and irritated. That is a normal feeling when we lose. Loss hurts, and it brings disruption and chaos into our lives. We have every right to feel irritable when we are coping with a loss. Acknowledge the feelings. "I'm irritable. I'm angry. I don't like that I've lost." Say it out loud. Give the feelings a voice. Expressing it will help it begin to disappear. Allow all the feelings to be okay. They are a natural part of grief.

Another of the psychological disturbances is being in a state of high arousal. It is a feeling of being on the verge of flying apart into a million pieces. At times it feels like panic. A way of slowing down that sense of high arousal, of moving too fast, is to utilize relaxation techniques. One relaxation technique that can slow you down is visual imagery. Visual imagery is a way of experiencing a scene by seeing it in your mind. We do this all the time. Have you ever been so thirsty that you could see a picture of an ice-cold glass of water? Do you remember being able to see the frost on the glass? That is visual imagery. When someone is giving directions, and they say, "You know where the gas station is on such-and-such corner . . ." you stop and picture that corner in your mind's eye. That is visual imagery. We can slow down the frantic pace of the arousal state by taking ourselves in our minds to a peaceful, quiet, tranquil spot.

Visual Imagery Exercise.   The best way to do this exercise is to talk these instructions into a tape recorder and play them back, letting yourself go through it. You can also read through this exercise and do it as you read.

Begin by assuming a relaxed, comfortable position, uncrossing your arms and legs, sitting comfortably in a chair, or lying down on the floor. Close your eyes and begin to breathe—in through the nose, out through the mouth; in through the nose, out through the mouth. Feel your body as it slowly begins to unwind, as it begins to slow down—breathing in through the nose and out through the mouth, in through the nose and out through the mouth, as your body is becoming more and more relaxed. Relaxing and relaxing—as you feel the tensions and tightness slip away—moving out of your body as you continue to breathe—in through the nose, out through the mouth, in through the nose, out through the mouth. And your body is becoming loose and limp—relaxing and relaxing and relaxing.

Now go to your favorite spot in the whole world—see it coming into focus as you arrive there. Take in all the details of this special place—the colors, the sounds, the smells. Enjoy it—enjoy being there—drink it in—feel all the good feelings that are held here for you. Soak them in—soak in all that goodness, all that joy that this place has for you. Become like a sponge, taking it all in, and stay with these wonderful, peaceful feelings—be there for a while.

Feel yourself relax in this safe place. Feel the peace here as you feel all things slowing down. Feel the safe center inside you—and as you prepare to come back, fill the straw basket next to you with all the good things you need to bring back with you—bringing back with you those feelings that you need—knowing that when you get back you will feel relaxed, peaceful, and in a healthy state of being. As you become ready, come back into this room, feeling the floor beneath you, and open your eyes knowing that you are feeling refreshed, relaxed, and at peace.

These are some of the ways, psychological and physical, in which you can soothe the impact of the shock phase of grief.

## SEARCHING/PINING

### What Is It?

Sitting at her daughter's grave, Louise felt as though there was no bottom to the well of the tears inside. Never had she felt such deep, intense pain. She came here nearly every day to talk to Jenny, to be with her. And every day she sobbed. It seemed as though that's all she did these days. The minister came to her house and asked if she'd like to go to church. She refused because she could not stop crying. She was torn apart inside. Her body shook as the next wave of tears burst over her. The days of her life began and ended with her heart aching for her lovely, lost Jenny. Sometimes she'd wake up in the middle of the night, tears spilling out. Her life seemed so full of pain as the rain continued to fall.

As shock begins to soften, the fact of the loss slowly sinks in and begins to be experienced, as our feelings break through. This second stage of grief is called searching/pining. It is at this time that reality gradually makes itself known to us. As our brief moratorium lifts, we start to feel the reality of loss and begin to deal with it.

Loss makes itself real to us as the awareness dawns that something is not right, that something is missing from our lives. We've known this in our heads, but now our hearts are awakening to the fact of loss. Events keep happening around us, constantly pushing the fact of our loss at us. Reality moves in closer and closer, steadily hitting home the fact that we did lose. And with the reality of loss comes its pain. Louise became aware, slowly, that she had in fact lost Jenny. Jenny was no longer at home. She wasn't there when Louise got up in the morning. Louise had to go to the cemetery to be with her, to talk to her. And as the loss became real, Louise ached with pain. In this stage of grief, we yearn and search for what we've lost as we begin to deal with the reality of it all. The symptomology of this stage seems to point to three ways in which we deal with the reality of loss: first, we seem to change focus; second, we search; and third, we look for ways to lessen the pain.

### Changing Focus

The reality of our loss seems to take over our life. Our world narrows as we change focus from the events in the outside world to attending to the loss and the events in the inner world of our thoughts and feelings. Symptoms of this stage that seem to indicate a change in focus are: a sense of preoccupation with the loss, with an inability to concentrate on anything except thoughts of the loss; withdrawal from other people and activities that normally give pleasure; loss of interest in appearance, and calling out for whatever or whomever we've lost.

*Preoccupation.* The instructor's mouth was moving, but she wasn't hearing his words. She was vaguely aware that he was writing something on the board, while clutching a stack of papers close to his chest. She checked her watch—7 P.M. She forgot to read what was on the blackboard. Seated in her usual place, first row, front seat, she was physically there. But she wasn't *really* there. She stayed inside herself. That seemed to be her whole world now. The rape had happened. It was over and done with. Bobbi was trying to forget. She didn't talk about it, yet it dominated her life. It was like a tape, replaying itself over and over. She was trying hard to forget, yet found herself trying to figure out why. Why had it happened to her? Who put the finger on her? What did she do wrong to deserve being so brutally attacked? It was stupid to leave the door open. It was all her fault. It had to be. She just knew it. She thought she should have killed him. No, she should have killed herself. She looked at all the mistakes she had made and wondered how she was supposed to live with them. She couldn't think of anything else. She'd lost her job yesterday—the third one now. Her boss had told her that she was preoccupied and making too many mistakes, so he had let her go. Sensing a presence in front of her she startled herself back. Class was over. She had missed it. Fifty-five minutes gone and she couldn't account for them. Confused, she looked into the instructor's face as she heard him asking her about the blank exam in front of her.

Preoccupation with our loss happens as we shut out the rest of the world while all conscious thought is tied up with going over the events leading up to the loss, again and again. We can't seem to concentrate on anything except the events of the loss, and our thoughts and feelings about them. Bobbi could not concentrate. Her attention kept wandering back to thoughts of the loss. She couldn't keep a job. She couldn't think about anything else so she stopped going to school. Her mind was totally caught up with the events and feelings of the rape. She was totally preoccupied.

*Withdrawal.* As the reality of our loss becomes more apparent, we tend to feel overwhelmed. We begin to withdraw, no longer call friends on the phone or meet with them for lunch. Life outside ourselves seems somehow unimportant. We forget about people and pleasure. We forget about ourselves. We are focused in our loss.

Louise peered out the window to see who was knocking on the front door. It was her next-door neighbor, wanting her to get herself together to go shopping. They had done this once a week, before Jenny died. Now, as the knocking became louder and Louise heard her name being called, she just wanted to run and hide. She didn't want to answer the door. She didn't want to see anybody. She wasn't interested in leaving the house. She wasn't interested in anything. She just wanted to be left alone.

*Loss of interest in appearance.* Along with the tendency to withdraw comes a loss of interest in our appearance. We forget to get dressed. We don't think about combing our hair or shaving. We are not concerned with how we look. We forget to notice. Our attention is not on how we look. We are only thinking about our loss.

*Calling out for what we have lost.* Changing our focus to our inner world as we move through this phase of grief, we become absent-minded while dwelling so deeply on our loss. Within this state of absent-mindedness, many people, especially those suffering a loss by death, find themselves yearning and calling out for the lost loved one.

In everything she did, Louise yearned for Jenny. She missed her so deeply. She'd call out for her as if somehow hearing her name out loud might bring her back. She spoke to the empty house about her love for Jenny and how very much she missed her. She'd forget to cook supper or pick up the kids from school. She was deeply into yearning for Jenny, calling for her, almost expecting her to appear.

### Searching

Whenever we lose something, our impulse is to look for it, to search for it. And so it is, also, with traumatic loss. Particularly with a loss due to death, people report feeling an impulse to search out parts of the environment that the lost loved one used to inhabit.

A tiny rocking chair silhouetted by the morning sunlight seemed to be waiting for her, calling out to her. Time and again, Louise would wander into the room, see the chair, and expect to see Jenny sitting in it. And then, the truth would brutally break through and thrust itself upon her. And she'd go through emotions that she didn't even know people had. It was the lowest point in her life. At other times, Louise walked into the room and saw the chair rocking. There was movement, as though Jenny had just gotten out of it. It seemed, sometimes, as though Louise were searching for her. In the morning she'd go into Jenny's room to get her up, and then remember, once again, that she wasn't there. Familiar routines no longer fit—only she didn't know that at first. It was as if she were unlearning her life with Jenny. She'd automatically fix lunch for her, and then be struck by another cold blast of reality. It was as if the reality kept hitting her in the face. Jenny was no longer here. Jenny was gone. Louise had lost her.

Suicidal thoughts often enter the mind of the grieving person in this searching phase, for suicide, in the case of a death loss, can represent a way of succeeding in the search for the lost person. The lost loved one would be found in a reunion with the grieving person in death.

For Bobbi, suicidal ideation was a way of rejoining her lost body.

Hanging up the phone, Bobbi could hardly comprehend the words that were echoing through her mind. She had lost the court case. She was confused. She felt betrayed. The district attorney had assured her that with the positive identification she had made from the mug shot, the man who had raped her would be convicted. And his words rang out again. She had lost the court case on a technicality. As she began to understand the impact of the words, she grabbed her keys and ran out the door. That madman was free. He was not going to have to pay for what he did to her. Then she was behind the wheel of her car heading for the river. Why fight it any more?

Bobbi had every intention of killing herself. This was it. It was all too much to deal with any longer. Her body was gone. It wasn't hers any more. That man's violence had taken it away. She had sensed that by prosecuting him, putting his body behind bars, taking something away from him—somehow that would help her get *her* body back. But he was free. She had no body, no place to live, no friends. Sitting on the riverbank, she told herself to forget it. There was just no use in living. She felt totally wiped out, exhausted. Without the physical energy to throw herself over the cliff, she sat there trying to figure out a way to do it right. She didn't want to botch this thing. Driving over the cliff seemed like one way to do it. She did not want to end up still alive. After all, she was already half dead. That was the way she felt. What was the use in going on? For what? Staring at the water, through her thoughts, her mind went off. It became blank. She sat there like that for a long time, and then began to feel a sense of peace, a slight sense of healing. Along with this came her realization that there was some other way of getting her body back. She wasn't sure how, but she knew she had to keep looking.

With all types of loss, there seems to be the need to look in some way for what we've lost.

The sun was shining into her eyes. She jerked herself awake. Stiff and aching from resting her head between the metal sill of the door and the rolled-up window, she gradually realized that she was in her car. Still not fully awake, Bobbi grasped at bits and pieces of memory, trying to make sense out of it all. What was she doing here? And, then, instantly, the familiar feeling was back. Fear gripped her chest as she swiftly surveyed the back seat and floorboard making sure that she was alone, making sure that *he* wasn't hiding, waiting for her. Panting slightly, she told herself to relax. She was safe. But that was the trouble. No matter where she was, she didn't feel safe. Her life was upside down. Nothing made sense any more. How was it that in such a short time since the rape she had moved thirteen times, sent Tracy to live with her brother, and was sleeping in her car. What was she going to do now? She knew that she was restless. There was this urge to stay on the move. If she stopped she might become the target for some lunatic again. She knew, vaguely, that she was looking for something. The rape had taken so much of her. She had lost herself. Her illusions about the world being a warm, safe place were shattered, were gone. She didn't even have a body. It seemed like an empty shell that she dragged along with her. It was as though it wasn't hers anymore. Her confidence and sense of control over her life were gone. And she was alone and shaky, sleeping in her car. All she wanted right now was to be safe and secure. That's what she was looking for. Being alone scared her and yet it was hard for her to be around people. She had no tolerance. It seemed that no matter where she went everything ended up in conflict. A few days after the rape, she had given up her apartment and gone to live with her oldest daughter. But she hadn't found security there, just slamming doors and misunderstanding. So she'd left. Then she stayed with a series of people that she hardly knew. There was no safety with strangers, just more hassles. On the move, too scared to stop, she looked desperately for a place where she could be safe. She had to find a haven, a safe place where she could begin to find herself. Her search for herself, her lost body, confidence, illusions, security, led her to a mountain resort.

Bobbi's search for the parts of herself that she'd lost began right after the rape. Her behavior seemed erratic to those who knew her. It was not like her to move around so much and then end up living out of her car. She was in the searching/pining stage of grief. She was searching for a sense of security. First she looked for security from her family. Then she turned to strangers. When those means didn't work, she looked for it in herself. Knowing that her car was not safe, she found herself a haven in the mountains where she could begin to look for herself.

Searching can come in many forms. The type of loss may be connected to the ways in which an individual searches. Sometimes the searching seems irrational and chaotic, and yet there still seems to be the need to do it.

Bill lay on his bed doubled up in agony. Here he was, once again in misery. Cathy had accused him of trying to destroy himself. Maybe she was right. Why else would he have eaten that Mexican dinner? The doctor had laid it all out for him, everything he could and could not eat. He knew that Mexican food was "off limits." And yet he'd thought that maybe, just this once, it would be okay. Eating had always been a vice with him. And now he was paying for it. Last week he had done a similar thing. He was well aware that stress aggravated his disease. He was limited to two hours of work per day. He was to slow down the pace and intensity with which he lived. Stress was to be kept at a minimum. But the case he had been working on was so exciting that he had lost all track of time and spent five hours doing intense research. At the time he thought that it wouldn't matter, just this once. The following two days found him sick and bedridden. Bill scolded himself. He knew better. He had been warned. So was he trying to destroy himself? He was really beginning to wonder. No, reaching down deep inside, he knew that didn't feel right. Then why was he doing the very things he was not supposed to do? He was playing the edge. There was a sense of looking for something. But what? What was missing in his life? His health—that's what was gone. Learning to live with this disease was what he was supposed to be doing. Yet it seemed hard for him to believe that he'd lost his health. He sensed a need to play the edge, to test it. That was it. Eating the wrong foods, putting himself under stress was his way of seeing if his health was still there. Playing the edge, he was testing the reality of it, just making sure it was real, all the while hoping it wasn't.

Bill was searching for his lost health. Continually, he did the wrong things to find out if the disease was still there. In testing to see if he might still be healthy like before, Bill was looking for his lost health.

Searching is a means of making the loss real. It is a way of becoming conscious of the fact that the loss really and truly has occurred. For when we search and we don't find, our loss becomes very real. We are then left with dealing with the reality of our loss.

### Looking for Ways to Lessen the Pain

The searching/pining stage of the storm of grief has two aspects; that of searching and that of finding. As we search, we begin to feel the impact of the reality of our loss. This reality brings with it severe pain. So we try to find ways to ease our pain.

Grieving people have reported different ways of finding.

Louise was standing at the stove preparing breakfast. "What is it, Jen?" She turned around. No one was there. Yet she heard Jenny speak to her. Louise was well aware that she was dead, but she could feel her right there in the room. This wasn't the first time that she had sensed her presence. She'd heard her before. She had even picked up her familiar scent on a few occasions. At first

Louise thought she was losing her mind. Now, in quiet acceptance that Jen was there in the house with her, she felt a sense of warm contentment.

Maintaining a sense of the lost person's presence, a feeling that he or she is close at hand, is one way that we lessen the pain of loss. Louise's description of this is a very common one.

Many who have lost a loved one through death experience hypnagogic hallucinations, in which the lost one is seen in the form of an apparition or vision. The vision seems to reassure the person that the lost one is all right. This eases the pain of loss. Finding through hypnagogic hallucination is not limited to loss by death. Bobbi began to find herself in this way, too.

Perched on a rock, surrounded by the flowing river, her tears fell freely. With her first bath in the mineral springs, feeling had flooded over her. At this health resort in the middle of the Sierra Nevada, Bobbi was finally able to feel again. She cried for the first time since the rape. She began slowly to sense her body as her own. The massages had helped that to happen. Looking up, she saw a vision of a lady. She instinctively knew that it was Mary standing there, carrying wildflowers that were magnificent shades of purple. Bobbi was more surprised than anything. She'd given up Catholicism years ago. And yet here she was, staring at the Mother Mary, wondering why she was here. The lady spoke of bringing her a gift. She talked of knowing what it was like to be a woman and to have lost something very precious. Bobbi understood that the gift was the lady's acceptance and validation of her feelings of loss. She was not alone. Someone else knew the pain. Someone else understood. Then, as her symbol of her own lost body and womanhood faded away, Bobbi began to accept and reclaim herself, her personhood, her womanhood, her own body.

Another avenue of finding is through dreams. Often, a message of reassurance and importance is carried in a dream. Some people who have had a loss by death report that their lost loved one came to them in a dream and reassured them that they were all right. Bill dreamed of the time when he was on the operating table—the time he lost his health. The dream carried a message of warning from his body.

Chills ran through his body. They gripped his heart, as he saw himself lying on the operating table. "This is what it's really about," boomed a voice on the loud speaker. Distorted faces looked down on him. One of the mouths mocked him. Moving in slow motion it whispered, "Hey, get real here!" He fought to wake up and another face swooped down toward him, haunting him. "Get in your gut, because you've already lost part of it. So get in touch with it!" The faces swirled and laughed and floated around the room. Fingers wagged close to his face. "Watch out, you'll be here again. You're pushing it, and soon you'll be here again." His body sat upright on the table, turned toward him, and mimed,

"You lost me once. Keep eating that food. Keep being distressed, and you'll lose more of me." And he was in his bed at home shaking and breaking into a cold sweat.

Bill's dream brought him a warning about "playing too close to the edge" with his disease. The dream served as a reminder every time he caught himself having notions about spending a week or two in the hospital being pampered. The dream gave him an important message, advising him how to take care of himself. It pointed him toward listening to his body and the messages it was sending. The dream was helping him to reclaim his body. Finding his body again helped to ease some of the pain of the loss of his health.

Catching a glimpse of a lost loved one on the street or in a crowd or getting on a bus, talking nostalgically about the loss, and going over painful memories of the loss are other ways in which people lessen the severity of their pain.

Sometimes, there is an attempt to make some kind of sense out of the loss by trying to fit the disruptive event into one's assumptions about the world. This is another way of recovering what has been lost. A friend of mine lost her twenty-six-year-old daughter very unexpectedly. She had survived bypass surgery only to die twelve hours later of cardiac arrest. Vivian was haunted by the whys. Why did her daughter die? Why did her heart stop? Why, after coming through surgery, did she lose her? She filed a lawsuit against the hospital in an attempt to make some sense out of this traumatic loss, to find some answers, and to alleviate some of her incredible pain.

According to Parkes, these aspects of searching and finding seem to be happening simultaneously. They seem to be inseparable.

## What Does Searching/Pining Feel Like?

In this stage loss becomes real. The reality brings with it overwhelming pain as the feelings of loss break through. It is a time of searing anguish. We are deeply hurt. Our bodies feel as though they've suffered an injury. It is as though something reached down inside us and ripped us apart. The pain that we feel is heartbreaking. Our hurt is so severe that we're not sure we can survive it. It is a time of great yearning for what we've lost. We feel distressed. Tears fall uncontrollably. Deep sobs wrench at our insides. We are in agony. There seems to be no bottom to it. We feel as if we will never feel any other way again. We never knew we could hurt like this. At times we feel angry because of what we've lost.

Most of us have never felt such intensity in our bodies and emotions. And with some of the symptoms of this stage, like withdrawal, absent-mindedness, suicidal thoughts, hallucinations, coupled with the intense physical and psychological distress, many of us fear that we are losing our minds.

"Mom, you didn't come and pick me up!" It was her daughter calling from school. Louise had promised her that she'd be there at 3 o'clock, that she wouldn't forget this time. And she'd forgotten. Now she knew she was going crazy. Nothing made any sense any more. It was just an effort for her to get through the day, to get up and shower, and get dressed, to remember to put gas in the car, to remember to turn off the coffee pot when she left the house. Her world had fallen apart. All her tears, all of these emotions were so hard on Dewey. She felt it just wasn't fair to him. He had loved Jenny as much as she did, and yet he wasn't falling apart. He was able to go to work each day. Why couldn't she do the same? Something was wrong with her, terribly wrong. She was a disruptive force in their lives. And she couldn't settle down and be a wife and mother. She puttered around with all this nervous energy and couldn't find enough to keep her mind occupied. That was the hard thing. She couldn't settle down and be normal. Nothing was going right. She felt as though she was losing control. She'd wake up in the middle of the night sobbing. At the supermarket she'd be going down the aisle and suddenly burst into tears. She felt spurts of anger. Her anger seemed to fly in all directions. Or she'd sit in her chair and just stare, for hours, losing all track of time. Life had changed. It was not anything like it had ever been. Everything was upside down. Louise was frightened. She was afraid she was losing her mind.

Louise wasn't losing her mind. She was passing through the storm of grief. She was right; things were not normal. Her life had been totally disrupted by her loss, and now she was attempting to deal with the reality of the loss. Searching/pining is one of the most devastating, distressing periods of grief.

## Some Ways to Get Through This Stage

At this stage of the storm, there is devastation and intense pain. Our lives have been shattered by the realization that we have truly lost. The reality of loss deals us a severe blow. Intense emotions overwhelm us. Most of the time we walk around thinking, "What am I going to do?" What *do* we do with all of this? Let's look at some ways in which we might help ourselves through this distressing time. Accepting the pain, facilitating our tears, assisting the search and recognizing a path for finding are all ways to deal with this part of the process of grief.

### Accepting the Pain

The pain involved in this phase of the storm is incredible. It is deep and it is overwhelming. And the acceptance of the pain is the main path through this stage. We must accept the pain and go through it in order to be able to let it go. If we don't accept the pain, it will remain buried inside us. It just doesn't magically go away. It stays with us. The only way it is released is by our moving through it and coming out the other side of it. So the passageway through this state is *acceptance*—accepting the pain of loss. That is not an easy thing for most of us. It is our natural tendency as human beings to seek pleasure and avoid pain. We are hesitant to let ourselves feel pain. This pain, however, must be felt so that we can move on.

Acceptance is all about believing and surrendering. It is believing in ourselves, in our ability to come through it—and through that belief, surrendering ourselves to the pain. So we must believe in ourselves and surrender ourselves to it.

Knowing some things about the pain will make acceptance easier. Knowing and accepting the pain and its intensity is normal, necessary, and healing. Understand that you are not crazy, you are simply grieving. If it seems too heavy to carry alone, then seek out counseling. Many people think that getting into therapy means that you're crazy or that something is wrong with you. What it really means is that something is *right* with you. Know that the hurt will pass in time, even though that feels impossible at the moment. Know that you can and will survive the devastation that you feel. Its severity will lessen.

Acceptance is about standing your ground and looking the pain and agony right in the face and embracing them. Acceptance is about being courageous enough to *feel*. Shutting off feelings, running away and hiding from them, does no good because the feelings follow you wherever you go.

People around us who care about us often cannot handle our hurt. When they see us hurting, they hurt, so they attempt to shut down *our* feelings. We must not allow others to shut us down. The main way that others attempt to get us to stop feeling is by invalidating our feelings. When they see our tears they may try to get us to cheer up. They may tell us jokes to try and make us laugh. They may ask us to look at the bright side of things. In doing this they subtly invalidate our feelings. The message is that our pain is *not* okay. Another not-so-subtle way in which people invalidate feelings is through ridicule or lack of understanding: "You mean you're still crying over that?" Another form of invalidation is the attempt to explain away our pain: "It's been six weeks since John died. Now you've got to stop acting like this and pull yourself together! He wouldn't want to see you like this. He's gone and you just have to accept it."

People who are invalidating us don't realize that by being *in* our pain we are accepting our loss. We're accepting it by going through it. What do we do with invalidation? The message is that we are not okay, that something is wrong with us. Don't buy into that. We *are* okay. The person who is invalidating us is having difficulty dealing with our tears. *They* are uncomfortable with pain. Their discomfort has nothing whatsoever to do with us. So first understand that you are grieving and that's okay. You are being where you need to be. When someone tries to encourage you to look at the bright side, let him or her know where you really are: "I know that you really care about me and are worried. I appreciate that. I'm okay. I just don't feel cheery. I'm hurting and I feel sad." Try to stay away from people who ridicule you. Tenderness and understanding is what you need now. If you can't get away from the ridiculer, make your feelings known: "I'm feeling really invalidated and I don't *need* that now. I'm hurting inside and I need to be letting that hurt out. So please don't invalidate me!"

When someone tries to explain away your pain, again let them know where you are: "I know it's hard for you to see me like this. But I am still feeling the need to grieve, and that's what I'll continue to do until the need is gone."

The way to keep from buying into the message that your pain is *not* okay is to tell people out loud what you are feeling and that it's necessary and okay.

Accepting our pain means getting into it and letting it flow out of us. This helps to ease it.

### Facilitating Our Tears

Creating an environment.    It is not always easy to feel pain. Pain hurts. Sometimes we hold onto pain because we don't know how to let it go. One way of helping our tears to flow is to create a soft, safe environment in which we can feel secure enough to release the pain. We can make this place within our own home, by ourselves, or with supportive friends.

Start with a room that is warm, a room that has a rug, pillows, or a cozy favorite chair. It should be a room where you feel comfortable and at ease. Close all the windows and shades so you don't have to muffle the sound of your pain for fear your neighbors will hear. Set up the environment so that you can weep, wail, or cry as loudly and as long as you need to. Choose a day and a time when you will be alone without interruptions. Take the phone off the hook so no one will disturb you. Dim the lights in the room or light candles. Select some sad, beautiful music and put it on the stereo. Any music that touches a sad note inside will do. Turn the volume up high so that the music fills the room. Make yourself comfortable, either by lying down on the floor or curling up in a chair, whatever feels best for you. Begin to picture your loss. Take in three deep breaths, breathing deeply and evenly, in and out, and in and out. Feel the emptiness inside. Feel what you're missing. Feel the pain. Feel it as it begins to move up and out. Feel the music. Take it inside. Feel it caress you. Allow it to touch the pain. Feel the pain moving, as you begin to let go of it. Just let it go. You may want to have a pillow nearby that you can hold onto it as you sob and cry. You may feel the need to rock. Do it. Allow whatever comes to just come. You may feel the need to say your thoughts and feelings out loud. Do it. Call out for your loss. Yearn. Feel it. Allow it. Know that you are healing within the release of pain. Feel the healing. Weep. Mourn, for you have lost.

If you can't create your own safe environment, then go to one that already exists. Find a group that deals with grief, a support group, where you can let it out. Grief groups are springing up in most towns. Your local mental health center, hospital, or suicide prevention line can refer you to such a group. If there aren't any where you live, then start one. I know three women who all became widows within a few years of each other. They all lived on the same block and they got together and formed their own widow's group. They nurtured each other and shared the grief together.

Keeping a journal.   Another way to help facilitate our pain and tears is to write in a journal. A journal can be like a best friend—something you can confide in, a means of sharing yourself without the fear of being judged or discounted. Keeping a journal can be a very powerful experience. Journal writing can help you to focus and integrate thoughts, feelings, and experiences. During a time when you are feeling disoriented, confused and losing control due to the intensity of your grief, journal writing can help you regain some sense of center. This will reduce some of the pain.

A journal is a place of reflection. Like gazing into a still pool, you can look at your thoughts, feelings, and experiences from different perspectives. And within that process, you can begin to sort them out. In this way, keeping a journal can provide you with a sense of perspective. Within the intensity of this stage of grief, a sense of perspective will help you to feel clearer. Rereading earlier entries also gives perspective. A log of your journey through grief can be very helpful. Being in your process, you may not be able to see an end to it. If you can see where you were a month ago, what you are feeling, the state that your life was in, today may not look as bad. With a journal, you can see your process unfolding. You can see movement. Seeing movement will help you to stay with your pain on your way through it.

Most important, by recording your feelings in a journal, you will stay in touch with them. You will stay tuned to your intuitional process, which will be telling you what you need to do to take care of yourself through your grief. Journal writing is a way to open blocked or held-back feelings. Recording your pain and tears helps them to flow. Many times I'll find myself crying as I write in my journal. In the writing, I've bumped up against some pain. The writing about it allows it to flow. Keeping a journal opens us up to ourselves.

Keeping a journal is very simple, yet it's the hardest thing in the world. It is simple in that all you need is a notebook and a pen. The hardest part is actually sitting down and making the time to do it. Once you have your notebook, date the top of the page. Just record whatever it is that you need to say—your thoughts, feelings, or experiences. Suspend all judgment. Don't look at what you're writing as bad or good. Just allow whatever needs to come to flow. Don't censor yourself in any way. This is your special place, just for you. So write whatever comes into your head. Try to write something every day. How much you write doesn't matter. Just put down what you need to say. Get it out of yourself and on paper. You can have dialogues with your loss. If you lost a person you can talk to him or her, or write him or her a letter—a love letter, or perhaps a hate letter. Say whatever is on your mind, whatever you need to say.

Creating an environment and keeping a journal are two ways we can help ourselves through the searching/pining stage of grief.

### Assisting the Search

Searching is what we do when we've lost. Searching gives us some comfort as we deal with the reality of loss. The following exercise is a visual imagery exercise that is designed to help us search. The best way to do this exercise is to tape the instructions onto a tape recorder and get into a relaxed position and take yourself through it. However, you can just read through it and write your answers down on paper. You might want to record your experiences with this exercise in your journal.

**The Search.** Assume a position of comfort. Close your eyes and uncross your arms and legs. Allow your body to begin to relax. Breathe deeply and evenly, in through the nose and out through the mouth and in through the nose and out through the mouth. Feel your body begin to relax. Stay with the breathing—in through the nose, and out through the mouth. Begin to feel your toes as they relax. Feel them go limp as the relaxation spreads on up to your ankles, and on up the leg, to the calf, as your body relaxes and relaxes. You can feel the relaxation moving up to your thighs, now into your pelvic area; all the tension and tightness is moving out and away from your body. Now feel the relaxation as it spreads into your abdomen and your chest as you breathe in and out, in and out. It moves up your fingers, up to your wrists and forearms, on up to your shoulders. Your neck is becoming very relaxed, letting go of any tension that has been held there, and the relaxation is moving up into your jaw. Feel your jaw as it relaxes and relaxes. Feel the relaxation as it moves up to your cheeks, your nose, up to your eyes and forehead, and all over your head. Feel your whole body now as it relaxes. Now all of your body is relaxed, and is relaxing more and more. Stay with this relaxation and feeling of peace and contentment for a few moments now . . .

Now, imagine that you are searching for something that you have lost. It is very important to you. You know that searching for what you've lost is very important, and that your life will be somehow incomplete until you find it. Where are you now, as you begin this search? Where do you go? Notice your surroundings. How do you search? What is happening to you as you look about? Notice what obstacles are in your way. (Give yourself a minute here.) Be aware of how you encounter these obstacles. And be aware of how you deal with them. What alternatives do you try? Now continue to search for a while for what you've lost. You may find that the search changes in some way as you proceed. Stay with this for a few minutes.

What do you find as you continue to search? Begin to find that which you've lost. If you can't find it, then imagine what it would be like to find it. Examine what you have found carefully—describe it in detail. See it, feel it, touch it. Be aware of your feelings toward it. Your loss has something to say to you. What is the message that it has, just for you? What does it say to you? Talk to it for a while. See if you can learn from it—take from it whatever you need. (Give yourself a few minutes here.) Now say to it whatever it is that you need to say—stay with that for a while. You have found what was lost—take this experience in (give yourself a few minutes here.) Now return to your existence in this room feeling refreshed and relaxed. Stay quietly with your experience for a while. When you are ready, open your eyes.

Now answer the following questions, allowing any feelings that you have to flow out:

What happened in your search? What feelings were aroused? What was the message you received?

How did you feel when you found what was lost?

What did you bring back with you that you can use?

This exercise works well with a group of people, also. Sharing the experiences can be very supportive and validating as you find out that others have felt similar feelings. This exercise also brings tears and pain. Allow them to come up and out.

### A Path for Finding

One way that we find is through dreams. In the case of a death loss, the lost loved one can return with a message of reassurance and comfort. Finding through dreams is not limited to loss by death. We can interact with all types of loss through our dream state. Bill encountered the lost part of his body and it gave him important information on how to live with his disease.

Our dreams are wise. They hold the solution to problems, new directions we need to take, and answers to our dilemmas. We need only tune in to them. You might want to record your dreams. If you view them separately, they don't seem to make much sense. But when you review a series of dreams, distinct patterns emerge. Sometimes we see solutions to problems presenting themselves in dreams. They carry messages for us. Recording them is a way of tuning in to those messages. It is possible to literally "dream up" an idea or solution. Dreams hold the key to dancing with our emotions. Feelings move about freely in the dream state, unbound by the judgment and censorship of our conscious mind.

They change, taking on different colors and hues. They seem to work themselves through. We've all had the experience of falling off to sleep restless, anxious, and unsettled. Then in the morning we are surprised when we awake with a sense of resolution and contentment. It is as though something was taken care of as we slept. While we dream our feelings are not bound. They bounce and skip and change shape. With the intensity of feeling that is tied to searching/pining, it is important to use the wisdom of our dreams to help us. We can follow ourselves into our dreams and bring back from them what we need. Finding our loss in the land of dreams, we can interact with it, work with some feelings around it, and find some comfort.

To do this, as you are in that twilight between sleeping and waking, suggest to yourself that you will find what you have lost and that you will receive and remember a special message you are seeking. Repeat this over and over as you drift, softly, into slumber. Your dreams will do the rest.

In essence, the searching/pining stage of grief revolves around searching for what was lost and in some way finding it. The searching and finding have the specific function of lessening the severity of the emotional pain brought on by the reality of the loss.

Mary heard the drizzle of the rain. Pulling back the lace curtain, she marked the path of a lone raindrop with her finger as it slid down the windowpane. With the dark night as a background, her aloneness suddenly struck her. A pang of anguish twisted within her as she now knew the truth of it all. Life was so unfair. Mary now stood alone in the world. Her thirty-eight years with Blas were gone. They were over. He was never coming back. Never again would she hear that familiar voice, or feel his arms around her. Never would she see his face again. A sense of despair filled her body. And this night seemed darker than most.

Unfolding through our grief, we come first to numbness, a place of calm and rest before the storm. Moving on into searching and pining, we encounter torrents of rain as we toss and tumble with the reality of loss. And now with the reality at our shoulder, we face the rumbling gloom of permanence and we sink into depression. We will now investigate the final stages of grief—depression and restructuring—in our quest to understand how we grieve.

## DEPRESSION

After we have become aware of the reality of our loss, the issues of its permanence begin to filter into our consciousness. The third stage of grief, depression, grapples with the permanence of our loss. It is here that we come to know that who or what we've lost is never coming back, that things will never be as they were before. What we have lost is gone forever. The way our life was, is gone forever. With the dawning of this awareness, depression embraces us.

### What Does It Feel Like?

The house rang empty. Louise sat paralyzed, staring out the kitchen window. The flowers in the back yard were in bloom. Funny how they always reminded her of Easter. Jenny had been here at Easter. She had run in with a bouquet of flowers, her Easter present for Louise. It all seemed so terribly unfair. Why? Why Jenny? Why her? Louise buried her head in her arms. Feelings of despair pulled her back down. As she thought about all they had been through, her insides ached. Five years of devotion and love from a special, beautiful child. They'd fought so hard. Even from the first weeks of life when they didn't know if she'd make it, and then through the handicaps and hurdles, they'd fought for her. And they were winning. She was blossoming, growing. When the leukemia fell on Jenny, Louise remembered how convinced she had been that they could fight that, too. They'd read everything they could get their hands on about the disease, determined to save her, determined to beat this thing, too. But they lost. Even though they'd done everything in their power, everything within their reach, they'd lost Jenny. There was no way to stop it. They'd been defeated. Jenny was gone and was never coming back. Louise despaired as she realized that she couldn't remember Jenny's face. Why? Why?

The depression stage brings an attitude of defeat and despair as we understand that our loss is permanent. Growing out of the sense of defeat are feelings of anger and guilt. Anger and guilt are the two most prominent emotions experienced in this stage. The anger is not continuous but seems to roll over us in waves. It is on and off. In a loss that is the result of a death, the anger is often felt as bitterness toward the loved one who has died and left the survivor behind. Many times the anger is directed outward toward the doctor or God or anyone who is close at hand.

Louise pounded her fist on the table, demanding an answer. All she got was silence. The silence seemed to magnify the anger that was rising inside of her. God had let her down. She had trusted him and put Jenny in his care and he had let her die. And those damn doctors killed her. It was all their fault. They had killed her. They had let her die. Plagued by these angry thoughts that seemed to come and go, Louise tried to get a grip on herself. And as the cat jumped up on the table, knocking over the box of cereal, she flew into a rage.

Guilt feelings often follow anger. We feel guilty because we have been angry. Guilt is really anger turned inside out. Shutting off the anger at those things outside us that caused the loss, we turn the anger inside out and it is now turned on us. Whether it is anger or guilt depends on the focus. If it is directed outward it is anger that we feel. Focused inward, the feeling changes to guilt. Focusing inward, we beat on ourselves for not preventing the loss. Blame for the loss is placed on us. With anger, the blame is put outside ourselves. Often it is a mixture of anger and guilt that we feel as we flip from one into the other.

The tinkling of the tiny wind chimes played through the air. Bobbi was staring straight ahead. There was a way to get even. Murder. She knew people who were willing to do it. All she had to do was say the word. The thought of him being tortured pleased her. She'd like him to hurt the way she hurt. Killing him, taking his life away—that would even the score. She wanted to see him dead. He deserved to be dead. He was scum. A bluejay perched on the railing, disturbing her thoughts. *Murder him?* Bobbi was horrified at her thoughts. What kind of a person *was* she? She had been enjoying the thought of *killing* someone. Something must be wrong with her. What a horrible person she was! She was as much of a killer as he was. What a bitter, hard woman she was becoming. She felt disgusted with herself. She was an awful person, just as guilty as her rapist. It had been her fault from the beginning. She had set the whole thing up to happen by leaving the door unlocked. It was all her fault.

It is a natural impulse to protest, to rant and rave when we lose. Bobbi's rage toward the man who raped her is certainly understandable. And so is her guilt. The anger seems to need to go out in all directions. We need to be in it, to test its limits. So we focus it outward at times, experiencing it there, and at other times turn it inward. Our anger needs to bounce this way and that. We need the directions of anger and guilt so they can slowly dissipate as we come to terms with the permanence of our loss.

Nothing mattered any more. Sick again, this time he had spent a week in bed. It was always going to be this way. Those days when he never thought about how he felt were gone for good. There was no way to bring them back. It was going to be like this from now on—pain, weakness, and exhaustion. It was just no use. Bill was sitting in the chair at the foot of the bed. He felt a wall of nothingness. He just didn't care any more. What was there to care about? Nothing mattered—not life, not people, not his job. Indifference was his companion. There was nothing he wanted to do. There was no point to moving, to even climbing out of bed. It had him beat. He couldn't fight it any more. He felt like giving up.

Depression is a time of feeling hopeless and helpless. We are helpless to do anything about our loss. And we have lost the hope that we are going to get it back. It is gone. We are defeated. Out of this attitude of defeat rises feelings of apathy. Bill felt apathetic and defeated as he realized that the loss of his health was permanent, that life as he had known it was no more. We get to a place where we just don't care any more about anything. It is a sense of giving up. Suicidal thoughts also present themselves here, as a way out of the defeat and despair of depression.

What does the depression of grief feel like? Within the defeat and despair are feelings of anger and guilt, hopelessness and helplessness and apathy.

## What Is the Depression About?

The evergreens loomed like giants reaching into the sky, emerald green against a magnificent blue backdrop. From the cliff she gazed at the rushing water in the gorge below. The swift currents took her thoughts along with them, flipping back through images, memories, feelings. It all lay before her—the rape, confusion, fear, pain, the lost court case, her rage, the guilt, her despair the night she'd been willing to give it all up and take her life. She saw it in its entirety. It was all crystal clear. She had lost. Everything was gone. She had tried desperately to find it all, to get it back in some way. But it was no use. She still had been brutally raped, she still had lost her court case, and the man still was free.

Now it was clear. Bobbi knew what she had to do. The time had come. Climbing down, she made her way toward a huge rock jutting out of the water.

On all fours, she stared intently into the moving river. A picture formed. It was the rapist. She peered into his face and looked deeper into his eyes. There was an icy coldness covering something. She peered intently—it was almost too hard to see. In his seemingly cold, insensitive eyes was pure terror. At that moment something gave. And she forgave him. All her feelings were swept into the river. She felt separate, apart. And she watched the water carry him downstream. She was finished, and she stood up and walked away, feeling light and tall, like the evergreens.

Depression is about two things: dealing with the permanence of the loss, and letting go. In coming to grips with the permanence of our loss, no longer do we search and seek ways to ease our pain. We surrender all efforts to recover what we have lost. It is in the depths of this depression, wrestling in anguish with the despair and defeat, that we finally let it go. It is here that we allow our loss to be truly what it is—loss, simple and clear—gone, never to return. It is a time of separation, a trying time, as we sever ourselves from our loss.

Bobbi had to let go of the rapist. He had become the symbol for everything she'd lost. She had to release him, so that she could move on. She had to let him go. For Bill, letting go felt like dumping garbage. For Louise it was the release of feelings of deep loss and regret.

The depression stage is about stepping back, accepting the loss, as is, and gradually turning and walking away. It is about unhooking—unhooking from the past, from the way it was, unhooking from the feelings around our loss, finishing the pain, the anger, guilt, despair, defeat, and apathy.

## Ways to Get Through Depression

Depression is the stage where we reach down into the very depths of our beings. Within these depths we interact with and touch some of the darker parts of ourselves. We encounter our anger. We confront our guilt. At times we bump up against huge brick walls that seem to block us. We also tap wells of strength, wisdom, and calm that we didn't know existed there. In our depression, we are struggling, fighting, and transforming. Going through the depression is necessary, for it is here that we begin to finish and reach a resolution. It is a part of our healing. As we move in and through it, there are ways to make the journey smoother. It is vital to keep the feelings of this stage in motion. Binding them will only intensify the pain and anguish. Facilitating our anger and guilt and looking at ways of letting go will help our movement through this stage.

### Facilitating Anger

Our tendency, during depression, is to shut ourselves and our feelings off, to turn our backs on them. It is very important to keep our feelings, ourselves, alive and flowing. In this way, given the space to *be*, they will work themselves through. Anger is a major part of the storm of grief. We blow. We gust. We rage. If we bottle it up, it will turn in on us and become destructive. Anger left alone to express itself is healthy. It is our human reaction to loss to protest. We have every right to be angry and to feel it. For we have lost. Our anger is necessary. It motivates us and pushes us toward changes that we have to make to grow. It keeps us moving. Violence comes from anger that has been kept in chains. So understand and accept anger as a friend. It is an ally.

Since anger is not one of the more socially acceptable emotions in our society, we may have to choose a safe place to allow our anger its expression. Or we may have to create our own secure environment. Check in your area for therapy groups that may deal with anger. If there are some, this may be a place to express the anger from your grief.

Creating a safe environment. Creating your own environment means finding a place away from others where you can yell and rant and rave to your heart's content without disturbing or frightening anyone. An apartment building is not the best place to do this, but it is possible. I managed to get away with this by warning my neighbors that I was going to be working with some anger on a particular afternoon, telling them that if they heard screams coming from my place not to worry, I was okay. They looked at me as if I had a couple of heads, but that was all right. At least the boys in blue didn't show up at my door.

If you know someone who lives in the country, this might be the ideal setting. Actually, you can use a room in your own house. As in facilitating pain, make the room a soft, dimly lit place, with a rug and pillows. Take your phone off the hook, and close all your windows tightly. Choose music that is loud—something with a lot of drums and bass. You can do this alone, or with friends. Do whatever feels right for you. Get a pillow and a plastic ball bat, or a tennis racket. A bataca, a padded bat that can be purchased in a sporting goods store, is ideal for helping release anger. Turn your stereo on high. The idea is to let the music drown out your rantings and ravings. Kneel in front of your pillow with the bat in your hand. Take a few deep breaths. Reach deep inside yourself and begin to get in touch. Where do you feel your anger? Allow yourself to feel it. Imagine it. Allow it to take on a shape or form. Feel it as it begins to move up and out. When you feel ready, release it—let it go through the motion of your body, striking the pillow. Use the force of your body to get it out. Let it come—let it flow. Verbalize it. Yell out loud the thoughts that are going through your mind. Scream—give it words, curse. Let whatever you are holding come out. Stay with it until you are finished.

Often, right under the anger there are tears. If you feel the tears, turn off the music and let them bubble up and out. You may have to facilitate your anger more than once as you move through grief. Do it as needed. Allow this for yourself. Understand that it is far better to allow the anger to come out in a safe place and in an appropriate way than having it sneak out in the form of attacking the ones you love. You'll feel better this way. Anger will seek expression. And you can assist it. When you take charge and help its flow, your feelings of helplessness and powerlessness will decrease.

Another way to help your anger to come out is to set up a situation in which you can scream and yell. The car is a good place to do this. Drive to a part of town that is not heavily populated. Roll up the windows and just scream, wantonly. Imagine, right now, how that would feel. Tempting, isn't it? Many times the screaming will change into yelling and cussing and telling somebody off. That's fine, just as long as it is coming out. Some people scream while they're driving on the freeway. This doesn't work for me because I can't drive and rant and rave at the same time.

Strenuous physical exercise is another way to drain off some anger. Pounding on a tennis ball or taking swipes at a punching bag works for some people. Use the way that works best for you. Work *with* your anger, not against it.

### Facilitating Guilt

Guilt is just anger wearing a different face. Guilt seems to be our way of handling the anger that we feel toward ourselves. Dealing with anger at ourselves seems to follow a pattern. Initially we feel angry at ourselves because we have erred in some way. In anger, at this imperfection, we disown that part of us that just can't seem to get things right. We slap our wrists. We berate and ridicule ourselves. We pout. We turn away from ourselves in disgust. Finally, we work it through. We cool down and begin to reclaim that part. We feel forgiveness for our imperfections and take that part back in.

In grief, we are angry for our part in the loss. We must have done something wrong, or it never would have happened. Perhaps it was something that we did in the past and for which we are now being punished. We pick some transgression and blame ourselves for causing the loss. We berate ourselves, seeing the fault as lying on our doorstep. Eventually, we begin to forgive and accept out part in the loss, real or imagined, as being forgivable.

We can assist this process. Our guilt needs to be experienced and expressed. It needs to be said out loud. So talk about the feelings of guilt. Say them out loud. Share them with someone who can just accept and listen. Another way to say them out loud is to talk them into a tape recorder. Or write them down in a journal. Since guilt is anger turned inside, try to get the anger at yourself outside you. Have a dialogue with yourself. Do the berating and ridiculing on paper. Become the part of yourself that is angry. Read yourself the riot act. Exaggerate it. Tell yourself off. Put it on paper or talk it into a tape recorder.

Now become that part of yourself that made the mistake. Tell the angry part what you feel and think about what was just said. Become the angry part. Answer. Let whatever comes flow out. Don't think about it, just let it pour out of you. Continue until you come to some kind of resolution.

Allow the part of you that is angry to express itself freely and openly. You can do this by asking it questions, by exploring it. Ask what that anger feels like. Describe it. Tell it to say whatever it needs to say to you. Ask what price it is paying for holding onto the anger. What price will it pay if it lets the anger go? Ask if it still needs to hold on to the guilt. Ask what you can do to help it release.

Holding dialogues with yourself and exploring the anger are ways to allow the wrist-slapping to happen, so that you can move on to forgiving yourself.

We must forgive ourselves for all the "shoulds" that didn't happen. We need to treat ourselves as we would another. When others make mistakes, we readily forgive them. We are understanding and kind. We need to extend that kind of consideration to ourselves, to forgive ourselves the way we would forgive another. Finding forgiveness in ourselves is sometimes very difficult. One way to find forgiveness is to write a letter of forgiveness to yourself. Start with your own name. Let the letter write itself:

Dear _____

I forgive you for . . .
I forgive you because . . .
I love you and accept you because . . .

Guilt needs to be felt and it needs to be expressed. But most important it needs to be released. A way of aiding that release so that we can accept ourselves again is to *refocus*. When you get to the place where all the "I should have's," "If only I had done's" make you feel as if you are spinning your wheels, that is the time to refocus. Instead of staying with what you "should have done," start looking at what you *did* do. Look for all the beautiful presents you *did* give.

Guilt is a teacher. It holds a gift for you. As you refocus, begin to look for the gift in all of this. What is the gift within your loss? What can you take away of value from this? Change from dumping on yourself to accepting yourself and your imperfections. Our mistakes teach us. Turn it into a learning experience. What have you learned?

### Ways to Aid in Letting Go

Letting go of the loss and the part of us that was tied to it is probably one of the most painful and difficult parts of grieving. Why is this? The difficulty lies in the fact that we must change. The pain lies in the acknowledgment of the disruptions in our lives caused by the loss. We need to make changes to stabilize our world once again. Change is difficult. Letting go is the first step in the acceptance of our loss and the acceptance of a different style of life. It is a giving up of the past and an embracing of the present. Letting go is crucial for our healing. We can help ourselves toward this.

One way is through the use of *dreamwork*. Just as we used dreams to help us in our finding, we can apply them to letting go. As you find yourself in that space of time between waking and sleeping, suggest to yourself that you will work on letting go as you dream. Ask yourself to remember your dreams. Repeat this, over and over, as you fall off into sleep.

There are many ways to let go. We practice doing so every day, though we're probably not aware of it. Throwing out the trash is a way of dumping things you no longer need. Some people, after the breakup of a relationship, eventually go through old letters and pictures that hold memories of the other person, and rip them up and throw them away—in a sense, dumping the garbage that they no longer need. Others burn pieces of memorabilia, the way they were burned. Still others flush away the crap that they no longer need. A friend of mine, once she had decided to move out of an unhappy marriage, flushed her wedding ring down the toilet. These are all forms of letting go.

Scan your life. What method is best for you? Maybe it's one we haven't mentioned. Find the way that works best for you. And then do it. Play with it. Make it fun.

Imagery is another way to work on letting go. The exercise that follows uses dialogue to help you finish with your loss, within the framework of a guided daydream. The easiest way to utilize this exercise is by talking it into a tape recorder and then taking yourself through it, as you play it back.

Letting Go. Assume a position of comfort. Close your eyes. Take in three deep breaths—in through the nose and out through the mouth, in through the nose and out through the mouth, in through the nose and out through the mouth. Feel your body relaxing more and more. And as you breathe, notice the areas of tension and tightness within your body. As you breathe in, bring the breath into a tense area, feeling the tension break up and move out as you allow the breath to flow out. Again, breathe into the tight area, and release the tension as you blow the breath out of your mouth. Stay with this a while, feeling your body, relaxing and relaxing. (Give yourself a minute here.)

Visualize your loss as sitting there, facing you. Take some time now to really see your loss sitting in front of you. Notice all the details about your loss, all the things that describe it—its color, size, form, shape. Notice how you feel about your loss. Where do you feel it in your body? Is there a certain area of tension? Notice how you feel as you begin to realize and accept that it is truly gone and can never come back to you. *Feel* those feelings—allow yourself to feel them deeply. Be aware of where in your body you feel them most. Let yourself experience any despair or hopelessness that comes with the realization that you can never have it back again, that it is really, really lost to you, that you can never see it, touch it, or feel it again. Be with that for a while. (Give yourself a few minutes here.)

Now become completely honest and open as you begin to have a dialogue with your loss. Tell your loss all the things you've held back from it, all the things you've never said before. Say these directly to the loss that is sitting in front of you. Express everything that comes to mind—resentments that you held back, anger that you were afraid to show, hurt that you never spoke, love that you never expressed, questions that you never asked. Be aware of how you feel as you do this. Notice if your body tenses somewhere. Stay in contact with your loss as you do this. Take a while to be with this. (Give yourself a few minutes here.)

Now *become* your loss and respond to what you've just said. Be what you have lost—how do you reply to this person that you've left behind? Be aware of how you feel as you do this. How do you feel toward this person that you've left? Tell the person how you feel, what your thoughts are.

Switch places again and become yourself. Respond to what your loss just said to you. Tell your loss how you feel toward it now. How do you experience your relationship? Now tell your loss what you need from it. Be aware of how you feel as you do this. (Give yourself a minute.)

Become the loss again. Reply to the expression of the needs and wants of the person you've left. What do you hear the person asking for? Now tell the person what you need or want from him or her. (Give yourself a minute here.)

Switch places again and become yourself. Tell your loss how you feel about it and what you think of it now. (Give yourself a minute here.)

Now *get with* what you know must come. Get with letting go of your loss. Tell your loss how you feel at having to let it go. Say whatever is left to say, whatever else you need to say. And as you feel ready, slowly turn and walk away, releasing the loss, knowing that you are letting it go on now. *Be with* how that feels. Allow yourself to feel it. Take this all in. Now return to your existence in this room. Stay quietly with your experience for a while . . . and when you are ready, open your eyes, and come back here.

Record what this fantasy was like for you.

How did you feel?

Where are you now?

Is it finished? If not, what do you need to do to finish?

These are some of the ways that can help you as you move through depression. The depression stage is concerned mainly with dealing with the permanence of the loss and gradually letting go.

# RESTRUCTURING

## What Is It About?

Louise unlocked the door to the office. She stopped and picked up the pile of mail at the foot of the door. Business was heavy this time of year. Leafing through the envelopes, she spotted the return address of the school. She'd gotten an A in her second semester of accounting. She felt pleased with herself. Her world was changing. It no longer revolved around housework and children. With Jenny gone and the other girls finding their own ways in the world now, Louise had been forced to look toward herself to find out who she was. Slowly she was piecing back together the fragments of her life, rebuilding it, a brick at a time. It had begun with her volunteer work as a teacher's aide. That had gotten her out of the house and around people again. A new friend who worked with her at school had suggested that Louise take a course to fill some time. She had never considered going back to school. She had no idea of what courses to take. Yet studying, learning, being in a classroom sounded like a good idea. Since she'd always enjoyed playing with numbers, she enrolled in an accounting class and discovered a special knack in this area. Her bookkeeping skills developed quickly. Louise still missed Jen and knew she always would. But now as she thought of her, it was with warm and happy memories. Jen had been an exceptional child. She'd been a gift. Louise felt lucky to have had her. And now her life was beginning to turn in new directions. Having started their own business, Louise and her husband had a lot of work to do. Louise's life was in front of her.

Once we've finished with our loss and set ourselves free, we shift into the final stage of our journey through grief. This is called *restructuring*. It is now that we begin the task of rebuilding our world, picking up the pieces that were shattered by the loss. Louise began to learn a new role. She was no longer merely a wife and mother. That role was changing. She began reaching out in new directions. In doing this, she discovered a new skill in the area of accounting. Being in school, she was meeting new people. And in starting a new business, she was restructuring her life.

In order to fill in the gap in our lives that was caused by the loss, new roles, new skills, and new behaviors have to be learned.

Like a jigsaw puzzle, the pieces were beginning to fit. Bobbi's world was coming together. And the exciting part was that she was becoming skilled at making it happen. When she looked in the mirror in the morning she saw a different person. The face staring back at her beamed with confidence and ability. She wondered what she'd learn today. Each day, she went into new, unknown territory, but she was finding out she could handle it. Taking charge of her life, she was getting what she needed for herself. She was becoming a forty-year-old woman, instead of the shy little girl she had always been. And she liked it. Yesterday she'd arranged a raise in her paycheck and additional job training. Her successes were small and yet they seemed so large. Looking back, she saw how far she had come. She was changing. Her life was moving. It scared her and excited her, all at the same time. The rape was in the past. She had so much to learn. Hope dawned on her horizon.

Bobbi was learning a new role. She was becoming an assertive woman who was developing the ability to fill her own needs. Taking control of her life, she mastered new skills and behaviors. Slowly, she was rebuilding her world.

Within this restructuring stage, our social activities have to begin again. It is a time of true acceptance of our loss. So we start reaching out in new directions, forming new relationships, trying new things, reorganizing our world that was disrupted by loss.

Bobbi quickly bolted and chained the door behind her and fell against it, slightly out of breath. It had taken all the nerve she'd been able to muster, but she'd done it. It had been really awkward at first, being alone, without an escort at the dance. She'd felt like every eye in the place was on her. A few conversations later, she began to relax. She even danced a bit. Going out again after so long had been frightening. Here she was, a rape victim, going to a dance alone and leaving alone. But it had been something that she knew she had to do. And to her surprise, she found that she could survive socially. Reflecting over the past months, she realized that she had been keeping everyone, men and women, at a distance. Now she saw how that had been wise. She was slowly choosing new friends, slowly building a community of people she could trust, confide in, and share with. She was putting the pieces back together.

With the acceptance of her loss, Bobbi now had the ability to start reinvesting herself in new relationships. She could now put energy into initiating new activities. Now that she was becoming whole, she had something to give, so social relationships began forming. In this stage we begin to put things back together.

## What Does It Feel Like?

If the previous stages have been worked through, then healing is nearly complete. It's not that we forget our loss, or that we wipe it totally out of our consciousness. We will think about our loss from time to time. But it will be remembered with warm and tender feelings, rather than with searing pain, explosive anger, or anguish and despair. As we reconstruct our world, we begin to feel a sense of balance, wholeness. We feel proud of our growth, and excited. We feel new.

The sunshine felt warm on Bill's face as he pedaled the bike along the winding mountain road. He sniffed the juniper in the air and drank in the shade of the tall green pines. A bird swooped by. Bill felt proud of himself. He felt the changes inside. Acceptance and peace were with him. He'd come a long way. A few years ago Bill never would have taken the time for a long bike ride through the hills. He didn't know how to play then. All he knew was to drive himself—to work, to achieve, to accomplish. Dealing with his feelings about the disease had been a lesson. He'd grown from being totally achievement-oriented to being pleasure-bound. Now he felt pleasure clear down to his toes. He had missed the beauty his senses could bring him before—the pleasant sensations they can bring. He had missed them because he'd been moving too fast. Learning to live with his disease was teaching him about himself. He was feeling balance now, a kind of wholeness. The part of him that he'd lost had never known the joy of play. That part of him had been stuck. Living with his disease was teaching him to risk. And risk brought with it adventure and newness. He was learning to be a different way in the world, and within this, his world was coming back together. He felt as one.

The feelings of this stage are positive as we feel the totality of our healing. Bill healed not only physically as he learned to live with his disease, but emotionally as well. The new person he was becoming was balanced and whole. These are the feelings of restructuring, the final stage of restoring our broken world.

## How Do We Grieve?

Riding through a storm that seems to force us through the doors of numbness and shock, down the hallways of searching and finding, through the cellars of depression, and up onto the porch of restoration is how we grieve. Padded within numbness, we huddle, cushioned from our loss. As it intrudes, we wrestle with its reality, wildly searching, and eventually finding, to relieve the severity of our pain. From the depths we encounter permanence, defeat and despair; and we painfully, unwillingly let it all go. Picking up the fragments, we slowly rebuild the ruins, and move on with our lives. This is how we grieve.

Louise, Bobbi, and Bill rode out their storms in similar and yet unique ways. Generally following the passageway of the stages of a storm, they each still grieved in their own special way.

Louise experienced shock or numbness in the form of hyperactivity. She couldn't slow down. She had a feeling of being on the outside looking in. Her search for Jenny was expressed in trying to maintain normal routines, such as fixing her lunch or going to get her up in the morning. When she couldn't find Jenny there, she went to the cemetery, sitting there day after day, talking to her daughter. Louise gradually found Jenny within the house by sensing her presence there. As the sharpness of the memory of Jenny faded, Louise sank into depression and defeat, knowing that she'd never see her child again. Anger showed itself toward God and the doctors. She was in despair for a time. But slowly, gradually, she was able to let go and sense a release of the feelings of deep loss and regret. Her world began to come back together as she got out of the house, and reached out in new directions.

For Bobbi, the shock took over her body in the form of exhaustion, insomnia, and emptiness in the pit of her stomach. She was frightened and frozen. Her search began with thoughts of killing herself so she could feel safe and get back with her body. Discovering that suicide was not the way, her search led her to a mountain retreat. Mineral baths, color therapy, and massage all helped her regain her body. Through the creative apparition she had of the Mother Mary, she regained her womanhood and personhood. Then, still plagued by rage, Bobbi fell into depression. She had still lost. The man was still free. Nothing was going to change that. Her anger showed itself in her fantasies of murder, and then she was left to struggle with guilt about the fantasies. In depression, she again had fleeting thoughts of suicide. Then, through the use of imagery, she let go of the rapist, her symbol for all of her losses. She freed herself of the anger, defeat, and depression. Taking charge of her life financially and socially, she began to fit the pieces back together.

Bill's shock took the form of irritability. Coming out of surgery to find he had lost his health was too much for him to take in all at once. Irritability came along with disbelief. It wasn't real for him. Since he couldn't believe that his health was gone, Bill's search took the form of "playing the edge," testing the limits to see if his health might still really be there. He did the very things that were forbidden, eating the wrong foods, deliberately putting himself under stress. It became apparent to him that the loss was indeed real. Through a dream he found a way to lessen the pain of the reality of his loss; he found the lost part of himself on the operating table. He gave himself a message of both warning and solution to bring back with him. Bill fell deeply into the apathy of depression as he realized he would never be like he'd been before. *That* Bill was permanently gone. Within defeat, he slowly began to let go of the old Bill. For him it was like dumping a lot of past garbage. He took back power over his body as he released the "poor me" feelings that he'd been carrying around. For him, a new life, a new Bill, meant learning to be a different way in the world. He learned to play and feel pleasure. And gradually, his life began to reshape itself.

We grieve by moving through a process of healing that is uniquely our own.

The sheer green curtains flapped noisily as the breeze gusted in through the window over the kitchen sink. The neatly trimmed hedges outlining the back yard caught her eye as she lowered the window. Stepping back in amazement, Mary realized that the shrubberies were her handiwork. Sure, her next-door neighbor had shown her how, but she was the capable gardener who clipped them regularly now. She did all kinds of things that she had never done before. As the bookkeeper for Blas' partner at the garage, she earned some much-needed money. She'd learned to spade the garden that Blas used to tend. She was so proud the day she'd picked her first juicy red tomato. And here she was, a woman in her sixties, who had faced a lifetime fear and had learned to drive a car. She'd even learned to check the oil. Blas would have been so pleased. She still missed Blas, but the pain was gone now. He'd always been a part of her. He'd always be a part of her. And with her days so full at this time of her life, she wondered how it was that she had been so afraid.

## HOW GRIEF GOT SCARY

Grief heals our wounds, and through it we repair the disruption of loss and re-build our lives. Why, then, are we so afraid of our grief? How did it become so frightening? Thinking about the cultural attitudes and messages that thread throughout our society can point us toward an answer.

## Cultural Attitudes

Our society has developed an attitude of avoiding and denying death. But it wasn't always this way. Years ago, people usually died at home surrounded by loving family and friends. Preparation of the body for burial was taken care of by family members; they bathed the body, chose the burial clothes, and dressed their loved one. This gave the family the opportunity to be with the loved one and take care of him or her one last time. It gave them time to finish, to say goodbye. Caring for the body in this way, the family could not deny the death of their loved one. It was real, though the reality was not yet felt. Within these rituals, a natural means for the flow of the tears and pain of grief was given. Death was accepted as a natural part of the life cycle.

Along with the acceleration of technology and progress in Western culture, the attitude toward death has changed. Death has come to be unnatural and unreal. The unspoken attitude is that death does not happen, at least not to each of us, personally. It does not touch us; it only touches others. Death has been put away into a compartment. It doesn't exist; it is not real. This is the way we avoid death. We live in a society that is bent on denying and avoiding the reality of death. Until very recently, death has been considered a taboo subject, one that should not be talked about. In many quarters this is still the case. This avoidance of death can be seen in a number of common practices.

Seventy-five percent of us die in cold, sterile hospital rooms. Our family comes to the hospital to visit us, not to care for us. They are in no way involved in our care. Much of the time they are given the message that they are in the way. We are separated from them by rules. They can only see us during visiting hours. Small children are barred. Much of our treatment is a mystery to our loved ones. With this wall of separation, serious illness takes on a sense of not being real. When the loved person dies, the body is whisked away at the first opportunity. It is as though the body of one who has died is somehow disgusting or dirty. It has to be swept away and hidden from view. There is little time allowed for the family to just "be" with their loved one—to touch and talk with him or her, to finish, to say goodbye. The body is moved to the funeral home; it does not go *home*. It goes to a foreign place—a place that is artificially set up to look like someone's parlor, an additional element in the sense of unreality. Disposal of the body—preparation for burial and the final ceremony—are relegated to trained, professional businesspeople. The necessity of tending to the needs of our lost family member one last time is taken out of our hands. If there is to be a viewing, the body is painted to look as though the person were still alive, with natural flesh tones and painted red lips. The body looks unnatural and erie in this state. That's because it is. We try to make the person appear to be sleeping, not dead. No wonder we feel uncomfortable as we look upon it. This is our denial of death.

Children are shielded and protected from witnessing death as if it were something grotesque, rather than a natural event in the cycle of life. Death, in our antiseptic, rational world, has become unnatural and unreal. Euphemisms are used to deny its existence. The denial and avoidance of death carries over to the attitudes and values toward grieving. A culture that denies death also denies grief. Death has become remote, forboding, frightening, repugnant, and mysterious. These attitudes toward death are reflected in the way we mourn. We no longer know how to grieve. According to Edgar Jackson, we have no meaningful social patterns for dealing with the feelings of loss.

> Modern man does not seem to know how to proceed in the expression of this fundamental emotion. He has no generally accepted social patterns for dealing with death and his rituals are partial and unsatisfying. His funerals are apt to be meaningless and empty. Either he is so afraid of normal emotions that his funerals are sterile, or they are so steeped in superficialities that they remain meaningless and normal emotions remain unengaged.*

I recently attended the funeral of a young man who had become so tormented and confused over his divorce that he killed his wife and then himself. With this double tragedy, I ached for expression of some of the shock and devastation that I felt. I had hoped that the funeral service would, in some way, touch my tears and begin their flow. The ceremony lasted about 30 minutes. I left the church feeling angry and empty because of its total meaninglessness. It had been cold and insensitive. This young man's name was inserted in the blank spaces within the context of the ceremony. It seemed that the ritual of the ceremony was more important than the tragic loss of the person. The words that were being read were words that were read in all funerals. They had no meaning. They in no way spoke to the life or death of the man who had died. The words were empty, cold, and did not relate to or touch the feelings of those who cared about him. With our attitudes of avoidance and denial of death, we've lost the knowledge of how to grieve.

## Cultural Messages

Cultural messages are unwritten "laws" that govern what is appropriate behavior and what is not. These laws are taught to us as we grow up. They are not always direct. Most of the time they are given in nonverbal and other indirect ways.

Three of these unwritten laws are that grief is time-limited, that it is limited to death loss, and that it is good to conceal grief.

### Grief is Time-limited

According to this "law," we are given a brief period to mourn if it is a death loss. The grieving period extends to three or four days, or until after the funeral. The message is that if we "fall apart" during that time period, our behavior is still within the appropriate range. Outside of that period, any outbursts of emotion border on the inappropriate. Once the prescribed mourning period is up, we are expected to be back on the job, behaving normally, while playing the charade that nothing has changed in our lives.

### Grief is Limited to Loss by Death

According to this notion, outward expression of grief is inappropriate for losses that are not the result of a death. The message is that the only time that grief is okay is when somebody has died.

### Grief Should be Concealed

In our society, grief that is hidden is admired and respected. Strong, stoic, emotionless behavior is praised. The message here is that showing the emotions of grief is a sign of weakness in character. If it is within the "correct" time period of mourning, this behavior is tolerated.

Breaking these laws, ignoring the messages, means that we are behaving inappropriately, so something must be wrong with us. Attempts will be made to convince us to change our behavior, with underlying questions about our sanity.

Slamming the car door, she peeled off down the street, tears streaming down her face. Bobbi had just had another blowout with her brother. He'd accused her of being "off the deep end." He demanded to know why she couldn't just pull herself together and be normal. Sure she'd been raped, but he saw that as no reason to quit work or not have a place to live. He wanted to know what was wrong with her. Everybody treated her the same way—everybody was hoping she would forget. Nobody would talk about the rape. No one would give her an ounce of room to cry or throw tantrums. When Bobbi did start to show anger, her older daughter had said she couldn't handle it and asked her to move. Her friends turned their backs because her strange behavior was uncomfortable for them. Everyone just wanted to put a big bandage on the situation. Bobbi was not supposed to feel it. Maybe she *was* crazy.

Grief becomes scary because we feel crazy. The cultural attitudes and messages distort reality and confuse us. We've learned from past losses. Outside us, society is laying down its expectations: Don't feel it. Don't show it. Act normal. Inside, we are devastated. Our inner world feels as though it is collapsing. It is sending us messages of deep pain. It pushes us to express it. Our actions are out of control. Outside, we are receiving one set of messages; inside, another. The result of these contradictory messages is that we feel crazy. Feeling crazy frightens us. We keep this with us from past experience with losses. So grief gets more scary along the way.

The attitudes of our culture deny and avoid death and grief. The cultural messages tell us when to grieve, how long to grieve, and subtly suggest that we hide grief. Between our own feelings and needs and the society's demands, our views of grief become twisted and distorted. These attitudes and messages rob us of permission to grieve. We are not allowed to grieve openly in this society. So grief gets locked away and hidden. Anything that is hidden away takes on more power and becomes scary. Grief becomes scary because of all the cultural limitations that have been placed on it from attitudes and messages. Grief has become scary because it's been forbidden.

## HOW NOT TO BUY INTO THE FEAR

Grief has become frightening for a variety of reasons. But there are ways to keep from buying the only fear: we can see the cultural messages for what they are; we can disregard the cultural attitudes; and we can sort out the contradictions.

### See the Cultural Messages for What They Are

The insidious messages that we get as we are growing up are a means for helping us to hide from death and grief. They are distortions of reality. Death is real. Loss is real. And our grief is real. In order to not buy into the fear, we need to call a halt to our belief in these messages. It is time to stop going along with them. They are potentially harmful for us. We need to take a stand. We need to look at and accept the reality so that we can have the ability to get on with our healing. The cultural messages are distortions of reality. Let's look at the reality.

The reality is that grief does not carry a time clock attached to it; we can't punch in and out within a prescribed period. *Grief is not time-limited.* Each of us is special and different. We each have our own unique inner time needs for grieving. No one else can tell us how long to grieve. Our grieving is an unfolding that flows within its own time. It can't be hurried. It can't be shackled. We need to take as much time for our grief as we need. We must follow our own unique process.

The faulty message that our culture has given us is that our behavior should be normal after a very short time. But our life space has been shattered by loss, so our behavior simply can't be as it was before. The reality is that our life changes and so does our behavior. The way that we repair our life is by passing through grief, and that means that we cannot behave as if our loss has not occurred. We need to mourn. We'll be numb with shock, searching, yearning, finding, despairing, and letting go. These are normal types of grief behaviors. Allow yourself to be there.

Another reality is that *grief is not limited to death loss*. Grief is the way that we deal with *any* painful loss. Any time we lose, we must grieve.

Reality is that *there is no need to hide our grief*. Showing our grief has nothing to do with the kind of person we are, or whether we are weak or strong. Showing our grief is part of healing. Concealing grief interferes with its expression. In hiding our feelings away, we hide ourselves. To hide our emotions is to discount them. Our emotions are *us*; when we discount them, we discount ourselves. When we are grieving, we need to be hugging ourselves, embracing ourselves, not throwing ourselves off to the side. Open expression of our feelings is vital. That's how we journey through grief and eventually emerge on the other side.

## Disregard the Cultural Attitudes

The cultural attitudes of avoiding and denying death are smokescreens. Denying it does *not* make it go away. Death is with us. It is an event within the cycle of life. To deny it is to deny ourselves a part in this aspect of our living. Disregard these attitudes about death. Don't buy into them. Instead, talk about death. Share your feelings about your own death. Share memories, feelings, and experiences about the deaths of others. Take charge of your own death while you are still alive. Plan your funeral arrangements now. Be involved in your exit from this world. Design your own ceremony or memorial service to fit you. What do you want said about you? How do you want to be remembered? What type of tribute would be distinctly you? Be the architect of your memorial. Make it meaningful. Make it speak to the person you are and your life. It is your final statement to the world. Allow it to come from within you. Allow it to *be* you. Get involved in classes that revolve around death and dying. Write your own eulogy, your epitaph. These are all ways to stop ducking death. These are ways to look it squarely in the face, to accept it, to get to know it, to integrate it. As we learn about our own death we are more equipped to teach our children acceptance and understanding, rather than ignorance and fear. As we become comfortable with death and reduce its fear, we'll also become at ease with grief and reduce our fear around it. Once we allow ourselves our grief, we can extend that permission to others.

## Sorting Out the Contradictions

As we grieve, we are receiving conflicting messages. The outside world, with its attitudes of avoidance and denial, is sending us certain communications. We're told not to feel, not to show it, and in some cases not to grieve at all. Inside, we are in shock. Our bodies are weak and wounded while our emotions are confused and intense. Within the conflict we feel trapped. The only way to free ourselves is to sort out the double messages. The first way to do this is to use the first ingredient in the formula for living with loss: *to give ourselves permission* to grieve. Since society isn't giving us permission to grieve, we have to give it to ourselves. Without permission, the natural healing process is thwarted. Giving ourselves permission to grieve cancels out the messages to the contrary.

In order to ignore those messages that work to inhibit our grief, we must tune in and take a stand with ourselves. We must be true to ourselves. We must accept and know that what we are feeling inside, where we are in our inner world, that this is reality. We must be true to what fits for us, what is right for us, even if it goes against the world outside us. *We must trust ourselves*, our instincts. Trust is the second ingredient in the formula for living with loss. Trusting ourselves is the component that carries us on as we ride through the storm of grief. What is trusting ourselves about and how might we create it?

### Trusting Ourselves

Trust is dancing with ourselves. It is choosing our own being as our partner. It is joining together with ourselves. Trust is dancing within ourselves. It is saying "yes" to our being, affirming our own inner wisdom and integrity. In the dance there is motion. The motion of trust moves us over the floor, dipping in this direction and swaying in that, never faltering, never questioning, analyzing, or judging. Trust has movements. It has steps. It knows where to take us and when. And as these once-inhibited steps merge together, the dance becomes flowing and fluid. This makes up the motion, and within the motion is a tuning in to the rhythm of the music. *In trust we tune in to the rhythm of ourselves—* our own inner rhythm that lies within our feelings and emotions. Trusting is dancing with our emotions. Being one with them, being in sync. Within this rhythm, we follow the lead of our essence, of our being. In following the lead we go wherever we need to go. Trust takes us by the hand and leads us. It leads us toward the things that we need for ourselves.

Trust also follows. It follows our own inner pattern that continuously turns toward growth, unity, and wholeness. We need only trust, and trust will guide us through the storm of grief. It will light the way through the darkness and gloom. It will take us in and out the doors that we need to open and close.

It will take us over the bridges that we need to cross, and past the byways that might distract us. It will take us down the pathways we need to travel. Trust will lead us to healing. We need only dance. Trust is the dance with ourselves.

Trusting ourselves is the channel for tuning in to our own intuitive wisdom. It is using our creative insights, perceptions, and abilities to heal ourselves. It is the way we find answers for ourselves.

A woman I know trusted herself. She had lost her baby at birth and her sorrow was deep. Within her was a sense of being drawn to the nursery, the room that her child would have occupied. She trusted herself and followed her instincts into the room. There she felt the need to rock. She spent hours in the rocking chair, off and on, for the next few months. And as she did so, her pain and her need to rock lessened. Eventually, she moved on and healed.

Trusting is finding our answers and the path we need to take, from within. When we trust ourselves, we toss the contradictory cultural messages out of our lives. They don't fit. We tune in to ourselves, to the messages from within.

## How to Create an Atmosphere of Trust

For trust to blossom, we need the right climate. We have to have the proper amount of light, water, fertile soil. There are two things we can do to create such an atmosphere: we can learn to tune in to ourselves, and we can weed our gardens of fear. Then trust is free to grow.

### Tuning in to Ourselves

Learning to tune in to ourselves is important so that trusting will be a natural, reflexive response. One way to open the channel into ourselves is through meditation. There is nothing supernatural or mysterious about meditation. It is merely focused concentration. In concentrating on one thing—whether it is a navel, a candle, or our breath—we shut out the rest of the world and begin to encounter ourselves. We no longer hear the dripping faucet, the clock ticking, or the motorcycle racing down the street outside.

As we focus our concentration, we close the door on the outside world and begin to turn our attention inward. As we do this, we encounter our chattering minds. Sometimes that chatter is deafening, as our minds go over things that happened at the office today, how we felt when the coffee was spilled, what might happen tomorrow. Soon our heart begins to race. Focusing through meditation is a way of quieting the mind and slowing down the body. Since we're not used to turning our attention inward, meditation is an art that we must develop. It is developed by practice. There are no shortcuts. It is learned through doing.

You need to practice meditation once a day. Put any expectations about it away on a shelf. Don't expect weird, dramatic, mystical experiences. It's not about that. Expect nothing. That is what the meditative state is—a place of nothingness. Just allow your outer self to be quiet, so you can tune in and get to know a deeper, richer, inner you.

Meditation is not difficult. Just find a quiet place, free of interruptions. Set the alarm on a clock for 20 minutes. In time, your inner clock will take over and you'll automatically know when your 20 minutes are up. Wearing loose-fitting clothes; sit in a comfortable position, either on the floor or in a chair. Be in a position where your spine is straight. Lying down is not recommended because the natural tendency, when your mind quiets, is for you to drop off to sleep. You want to *be* there, conscious, for the meditation state.

Now, begin counting your breaths. One, as you breathe in, two, as you breathe out, three, as you breathe in, four, as you breathe out, counting up to ten. When you reach ten, go back to one. Do this over and over, counting your breaths from one to ten and back to one again. Keep your attention focused on your breathing. Other thoughts will try to break through such as how you have to pick up your laundry before five. Allow these thoughts to come into your mind and pass through as you continue counting your breaths. From time to time you will notice that you are on number twenty-eight, or forty-two. Your concentration has strayed. Your attention from counting to ten has gone away. This will happen. There's no problem. Just bring yourself back to one and begin counting your breaths up to ten again. It will become easier each day. Each day you will reach new levels as you begin to touch and know parts of yourself. As you learn to focus, shutting out the hustle and bustle of the outside world, and quieting the chatter on the inside, your mind will empty itself. It will become silent and blank. It will become still and calm.

It is within the silence, within the blank mind, that your inner being will show itself. It is here that you will become merged as one. It is here that you will resonate with yourself. Meditating for 20 minutes each day will take you here, where you will be in tune with yourself. Remember, meditation is an art that has to be developed, not a miracle that falls out of the sky.

### Weeding Out the Fear

The soil that keeps trust from growing is one that is full of weeds of fear. Fear wraps itself around the roots of trust and destroys it. Fear keeps trust away. So weeding your garden of fear is a means for creating the soil for trust. Some ways to weed your garden are to explore your catastrophies and to use imagery to help you release fear.

Fear comes from unknowns. When we keep things unknown, they take on more power and become bigger. They grow. Taking a good hard look at our fears puts them in perspective. It's like popping a giant balloon with a needle. As the air escapes, the balloon changes size and shape. It falls away to nothing. Looking at the catastrophies around our fears is one way of taking the air out of the balloon. To look at catastrophies, we first have to name them, to narrow them down to one fear. Then we think about the catastrophe around it. What is the worst possible thing that can happen? As that answer comes up, get into the catastrophe around it. Here's an example of how this works:

> *Name the fear:* I'm afraid of writing this book.
>
> *Get into catastrophe:* What's the worst possible thing that could happen about writing this book?
> The worst thing that could happen is that nobody will like it.
>
> *Get into catastrophe:* What's the worst possible thing about that?
> The worst possible thing about that is that it means I'm worthless, no good. That I'm a failure.
>
> *Get into catastrophe:* What's the worst possible thing about being a failure?
> The worst thing about being a failure is that I won't try again.
>
> *Get into catastrophe:* What's the worst possible thing about not trying again?
> The worst thing about that is that I'll be stuck.
>
> *Get into catastrophe:* What's the worst possible thing about being stuck?
> The worst thing about being stuck is that I'll have to look in new directions. I'll have to make some changes. I'll have to grow.

The fear loses all its emotional charge as its catastrophies are explored. It's been reduced, put into perspective. It's not even negative. Exploring possible catastrophies showed me the way out if my worst fears were to come true. That didn't leave much for me to be afraid of. And then I no longer had excuses for not writing this book. When you explore possible catastrophies, just go with the first thing that comes to your mind. Don't analyze it. Don't judge it. Just flow with it. Sometimes the absurdity of our fears makes itself known, and that can be fun. The main thing this exercise does is to help you put fear into perspective so that it no longer paralyzes you.

The use of imagery is a different level where we can work on fear and release it. In imagery we symbolically meet with our fears, explore them, and then allow them to go. In the following exercise, we'll put ourselves into a relaxed state and move through the guided daydream. Recording the instructions on a tape recorder, and then playing the tape back as you take yourself through it is one way to do this exercise. Reading, and noting your experience on paper as you go along, is another way.

The hot-air balloon. Find yourself in a position of comfort, uncrossing your arms and legs. Take in deep breaths, in through the nose and out through the mouth, in through the nose and out through the mouth. Feel your body as it begins to relax, as it relaxes more and more. As you continue to breathe, in through the nose and out through the mouth, feel the areas in your body where there is tension. As you continue to breathe, deeply and evenly, feel the tension and tightness melt away as your body becomes loose and limp, relaxing and re-laxing and relaxing. Stay with this for a while. (Give yourself 30 seconds of blank tape time.)

Now imagine yourself in a lush green meadow, surrounded by brilliantly colored wildflowers growing all around. Take your shoes off and feel the damp-ness of the cool green earth as it rises up and caresses your feet. Feel the light breeze dance by as it brushes up against your cheek. Soak in the gentle warmth of the sun on your shoulders and arms. Sniff the aromas of spring, the scent of freshly cut grass, the perfume of flowers, the crisp freshness of the clean air. Enjoy the calmness of it all as you take some time to drink all this in. (Give yourself a few minutes of quiet tape time.)

Now, notice a form in the distance—the shape of something you cannot clearly make out. Begin moving toward it and as you do, see it as it comes into focus. Realize that sitting here in the center of this lovely field is a large hot-air balloon. Coming close, start to examine it—its size, its texture, its colors. What is it made of? Notice a chute that runs down into the basket of the balloon, and read the sign on the chute that says: "Put your fears here." And now begin to search deep, down inside yourself and pull out, one by one, all the things that you are afraid of—all the things that keep you trapped, all the things that stand between you and your inner self. Place them one by one on the ground in front of you. Now choose the one that draws you toward it. Begin to look closely at it. What does it look like? How large is it? What shape does it take? What is its color, its texture? Give this fear a name. Now place it back on the ground and pick up your next fear. Examine it, giving it form, shape, color, size, and texture. Give it a name. When you've become acquainted with it, lay it down. Continue to do this with each and every fear that you carry. Look at them, touch them, and then lay them on the ground before you. Be aware of how you feel as you do this. Where are those feelings in your body? (Give yourself 2 minutes of blank tape time.)

Now go to each fear, one by one. Ask it what its function is. Why is it with you? Ask if you still need to carry it. If you don't, then send it down the chute into the hot-air balloon. Take some time now to do this with each fear. (Give yourself a few minutes.)

Now look down at the ground. If there are still some fears there that you need to carry, take them back into yourself knowing that they no longer will be in your path, blocking you in any way. Now untie the rope that holds the balloon to the earth and watch as the enormous balloon slowly lifts itself off the ground. Continue to follow it as it ascends, higher and higher into the sky, carrying away with it all of the fears that you no longer need. See it as it floats, flies, and drifts up higher and higher into the heavens, as it becomes smaller and smaller—so small that it is just a tiny dot way up in the sky. Be aware of how you feel as you let go of these fears. Be with this for a while. (Give yourself a minute of tape time.)

When you're ready, come back into this room feeling very light and refreshed. When you feel ready, open your eyes and sit up.

Describe what this was like for you.

What feelings did you experience?

What did you find out about yourself? About your fears?

Where are you now? What are you feeling with yourself?

Tuning in to ourselves and wiping away our fears creates an atmosphere for trust. Trust is a vital ingredient in the formula for living with loss. Trust is tuning in to the inner self—the one that can take us down the paths we need to travel for passing through the storm of grief.

Permission, the first ingredient in the formula *allows* our grief. Trust, the second ingredient, *affirms* it.

The short, staccato buzzes sounded strange and aloof as the long-distance operator put the call through. Hawaii was far away from the bed of her mother. Darlene had joined her husband on R & R from his tour in Vietnam. But she wasn't there really. Her mind and heart stayed with her mother, who she knew was dying. It seemed as if they'd never gotten a chance to say goodbye before she left. Darlene felt unfinished. So every night she phoned from the islands and every night she was told that her mother was finally sleeping and could not be disturbed. It was bad. Her condition was deteriorating.

Darlene thought back to when it had all begun. Her sister Kathy was pregnant and was getting married soon. That was when her mother had started drawing the drapes during the day, closing up inside, shutting out the world. Soon after that she seemed to be sick all the time. They thought it was the flu, until the diarrhea, nausea, and rapid weight loss became constant. Darlene's mother grew weaker and thinner. And she refused to confide in anyone. She would not tell the doctor how sick she was. Finally, with the diagnosis of cancer, she became even quieter. It was as though she were giving up. Then, toward the end, with tubes snaking in and out of her, she could not rest. She was never at peace; there was a constant stream of babbling that no one could understand.

Darlene's heart was heavy with the injustice of this suffering. She felt heavier as she realized that they had never spoken of her dying. Darlene cradled the phone for a minute as she sorted it through. Her mind was made up. She dialed the airlines and made a reservation. Her aunt met her at the airport and they took her mother to the hospital for the final time.

Behind the thunder, resonating from our loss, is the raging fury of the storm that is grief. And this storm moves us through a natural process that in time unifies our lives. As a loved one is dying from terminal illness, our losses begin immediately and we enter grief's door even before our loved person is lost forever to death. Our grief is not static. It is in motion. Darlene sensed the thunder of her mother's death. She followed her intuition and flew home.

A third ingredient in the formula for living with loss is *flow*—flowing with and through the feelings of grief. In the course of this chapter, we'll look at what flow is, its importance, and what happens if we don't flow with our grief.


## WHAT IS FLOW?

Flow is movement. It is the motion of the dance. In trust, we embrace our feelings and say "yes" to ourselves. We dance. In flow, as we go with our feelings and follow their lead, we move with the dance. Flow is the motion of the dance. It is easy, gentle movement.

To flow with ourselves is to move in and under and through our grief. This flow is smooth, sweeping motion, in no way rough, choppy, or hesitant. It is unencumbered.

Flow is sliding gently in step with our inner beat, the inner rhythm of our feelings. Emotion is the *movement of feelings*. Within flow we fall in time with that motion and follow wherever it leads, whether it is into the depths or up to the heavens. Flow is following that motion through heavy turbulence or into gentle, still nights. It is going with the direction of our feelings, wherever they may take us.

Flow is moving in the oneness of all that we are. It is every part of us, moving together as one. It is a connection to and with ourselves. As in dance where our bodies, minds, feelings, spirits glide as one, so it is within flow. Our mind, bodies, spirits, and feelings move together, not pushing against one another or pulling away from each other—just a movement in unison, in one motion.

Flow is the movement of growth, of becoming. It is a stream—yielding, tumbling, widening, narrowing, raging, passing—becoming the ocean.

Flow is not bound up or tied down. It is not tied to ideas, expectations, achievements, or goals. It is not future-bound. It is *now*. Flow is being, being in the motion, the current, the now. It is being in the now feeling, going with it as it is in passing. Flow knows no *boundaries;* it is simply motion.

Flow is free. It is free of masks, insecurities, worries, anxieties. It is free of the unnecessary, the trivial, the unimportant. It walks naked.

Flow is tuning in to our own natural direction and going down the paths that we need to take. It is moving with our inner magnet, being drawn toward, being pulled forward.

Flow happens as we follow, as we join in and go with. It happens as we join in and dance. Flow is the movement of the dance.

## How Does it Feel?

Flowing with ourselves feels like white billowing clouds, drifting across a sea of blue sky. It is unencumbered motion. Flowing is free and uninhibited.

Within flow is the feeling of oneness, of belonging. Flow connects us with ourselves and with nature around us.

Flow feels light. It is not weighed down by the anchors of judgments, analyses, or questions.

Flow feels nurturing. Even as we sob with the deep tears of grief, the flow of these feelings as they move up and out is healing. We feel cared for as we nourish ourselves, our feelings. Within our anger, as we flow with the rage over our loss, the motion of the anger feels like relief. We feel lightness as the bitterness leaves. Flow feels right. It feels right in the center of our being.

These two ingredients of trust and flow are like silver and gold threads that are woven together. One needs the other. They work within each other. We need to embrace ourselves and say "yes" so that we can go along, and we need to go along as a part of embracing. Trust is the dance with ourselves, and flow is the movement within the dance.

## WHY IS FLOW SO IMPORTANT?

Flowing along with our feelings is a vital ingredient for living with loss. Why is this so?

Flowing with our feelings helps us to define reality. Feelings define reality. Many Americans felt that the war in Vietnam was inhumane and wrong. They felt appalled at killing other beings. And when thousands took to the streets questioning the country's involvement, voicing their feelings, more and more people gradually began to feel that the war was wrong. The reality that had been in the country was that our involvement in a war there was right. Many people felt good about that, and most of America supported the war. Young men joined the armed forces to go and fight the good fight. But as feelings changed, the *reality* began to change. The mood, the flow of feelings of the country, changed; public opinion swung from supporting the war to opposing it. Some of the men in the armed forces began to refuse to fight. Others refused to answer the call of the draft. The flow of the feelings of the people in this country defined the reality. We've all experienced times in our lives when we've sensed that someone was lying to us. There probably was no visible proof to the contrary, but inside we knew that what was being said was not true, was not real. And the reason that we knew that was because of a stirring, a movement of feeling in our gut that told us so. Feelings define reality. Feelings *are* reality.

We all can remember moments when we've wanted to kick ourselves for not following our intuition, another word for feelings. When we stay in touch with intuition, we know clearly the reality of any situation. Flowing with our feelings is a way to define reality. In a world that changes as rapidly and haphazardly as ours, it is often difficult to know what is real and what isn't. Who or what do we believe when leaders are telling us opposite "truths"? We become confused, and hence, vulnerable. Being able to define reality is important so that we can find our way out of confusion. It is a way that we take care of ourselves so that in our vulnerability, we're not used and abused.

In grief, during a time of devastation and pain, we are often dealing with different sets of messages. One set is our feelings, telling us that we are hurt, shattered, angry. The other set is messages from outside, urging us not to feel, telling us that our feelings are invalid. And within this bind we feel more distressed and confused. We begin to feel crazy. We're not sure what is real. Flowing with our feelings and following them gives us a way out of this bind. Flow gives us the reality of this conflict. And within the reality we start to find what we need to do to take care of ourselves. So *defining reality is important.*

Feelings are real and they are us. So when we are in the flow with our feelings we are real. We are not hiding behind a phony mask saying one thing while feeling another. We are honest, we are real. When we are real, others can touch us, connect with us, and comfort us. When we are real, we're open and we can take in the gifts that others are waiting to give us.

Flowing with our feelings not only keeps us connected to others, it makes us whole. When we inhibit flow we are incomplete and split apart. We have declared war on ourselves. We've all seen the caricature of the movie hero, the lone scientist, who devotes himself to his lab and his work, living in a world devoid of feelings. Feelings do not exist for him. He locks them tightly away and cold, hard logic is what he worships. He seems split. He appears to live from the head up. And there the battle lines are drawn. The body is tightly defending as he struggles to hold back the flow of feelings. He stands straight and moves with tautness. There is no grace in his motion. His movements are wooden and mechanical. Serious in nature, he hides in his work away from feelings. He hides out in formulas and equations. Half of him seems to be missing. There is no spark. There is no pleasure, softness, sensitivity. His face is drawn into a skeptical scowl. Rarely does he laugh. He doesn't know humor; it is foreign to him. There is no lightness in his step. He lives in the upper part of his body. He stays in his head. He has become only his intellect, only his head. His heart is missing. His heart, the house of his feelings is closed down and locked tight. He is at war with himself. Dragging through life he is half, not whole, out of step, off-balance. Major parts of him are buried in a deep grave.

In order to be whole we need to be integrated. Every part of us needs to be accepted and cherished. Every part needs expression. When we are whole there is no tug-of-war yanking this way and that for control. There is no fortress walling parts of us away. There is no conflict. No part of us is buried. When we are whole, all parts of ourselves are available to us. Sometimes the situation calls the logical, analytical side into action. At other times, our soft, tender, and creative side is needed to play and dance and sing. Being whole is important. When we are whole we have access to all parts of ourselves. During a time of loss we need to be able to nurture ourselves. We must have the ability to call in that part that knows how to nurture, to care for us. It is within wholeness that this can happen. When we are whole we have more to give, both to ourselves and to others.

The best way to get good things for ourselves is to give good things away. In order to receive something of value, we first have to give it away. If, from our wholeness, we can give away tenderness and care, we'll get tenderness and care back. If we can share and give away the different parts of ourselves, then we get them back. In this interchange of giving and getting is the quality, the fullness, the richness of life. Being whole is important for the quality of our lives and the quality of our grief.

Flowing with our feelings makes us human. It is in our feelings that we find our humanity. We are more human when we air our vulnerability, our anger, than when we mask them. Wearing our mask, pushing our feelings out of the way, cutting them off, we become empty and cold. We become like a machine, a robot that walks and talks and goes through the motions, but that isn't human. Our feelings are our humanity. When we're out of sorts with our humanity we lose warmth. We run cold. As we run cold, we lose the connection to ourselves and others. As the richness and fullness of our lives are lost, we become blunted. Moving through life we miss it—we miss both the roses and the thorns. We pass it all by; we miss out on ourselves, losing our humanity, our ability to feel and connect. We no longer see people as other human beings. Wars, riots, murders, are the results of our loss of humanity. So it is important to feel, to be human, to be connected.

We must flow with our feelings, because that is what keeps us alive. When we don't feel anything, we lose heart. We become heavy. When we cut off one feeling, we trap them all. Shutting down the pain of loss also bars feelings of joy and contentment. When we attempt to remain immune to the flow of our feelings, we begin to feel nothing. We become like a turtle lumbering through life, carrying the heavy, empty shell; we don't live, lose, love, or laugh. We just exist. When we feel nothing, our world becomes nothingness; we experience deadness. As a person starts to feel dead inside, life loses meaning. As life becomes meaningless, empty, the person sees no purpose, no reason to go on living. And the stage is set for self-destruction.

It is vital to flow with our feelings, for their movement is our life force. The flow of our feelings keeps the flame burning brightly inside. We may be seething with rage or suffering with the pain of loss, but it is within that pain, within that rage, within that flow of *feeling* that we know, without a doubt, that we are alive. Sometimes being alive means tears and hurt. Other times it means roaring with laughter and joyful play. The flow of our feelings, whether they hurt or tickle, is life. Flowing with our feelings makes us alive, whole, connected, real human beings. And these are the reasons why flow is so very important.

## WHAT HAPPENS IF WE DON'T FLOW WITH THE FEELINGS OF GRIEF?

The storm of grief carries with it the rain of tears, anguish, and pain; it brings the dark, threatening clouds of anger, guilt, and despair. It is the storm that we pass through to become whole and alive again. In going through it, the sense of sorrow and loss, feelings of rage and abandonment have to be felt and expressed. Fears of insanity, guilt, and hostility have to be dealt with to allow healing to take place. Our healing comes from flowing with the feelings of grief. But what if that flow is stopped? What if we put our feelings aside or bury them away?

If we bury our feelings of grief and stop their flow, the grief work comes to a screeching halt; the purpose of grief is not realized. Grief has a special purpose. Loss is the deprivation of something that was valuable to us. It is the sense of something of value being stolen away from us. Value comes from the amount of ourselves, the energy, that we've invested in a particular person, place, or thing. It is through this bond of our energy that we become attached. In loss, we lose not only that cherished person, place, or thing but also the part of ourselves, our energy, that tied us to it. The special purpose of grief is that it enables us to unlearn our attachment to what we've lost; this frees up the energy, the part of ourselves that was invested there. Through the process of grieving, we search, we find, we let go. In letting go of the loss we let go of the energy that was bound up with it. This energy is then available to us to be put in new directions for our growth and well-being. We use this freed-up energy to rebuild our lives, to take us back to a place of wholeness. If we do not flow with our feelings of grief, then grief stops, and a thick mire immobilizes us.

As a storm rages on, it can create pools of deep mud that stop movement. In the storm of grief, also, there exists the possibility of mire forming. Stopping the flow of our feelings of grief will stop movement through the process. Our grief will stop. We will fail to "unhook" from our loss, and the energy that was tied up there will become dammed. Rather than passing through grief, we will become stuck in its mire.

The mire is created as we attempt to avoid the feelings and distress tied to grieving. As the natural feelings of mourning are denied, shunned, or locked away, the flow of our process of unfolding is interrupted, and the consequence is a disturbance in the normal process of grief. Within the mire, the disturbance takes two forms: *delayed* and *distorted* grief reactions. Erich Lindemann observed these reactions in his study of the Coconut Grove disaster victims;[1] we will discuss them in the following sections.

## Delayed Grief Reactions

Delayed reactions seem to involve the putting away of our feelings on a shelf, putting our grief "on hold." This may involve a situation in which we are confronted with important tasks that demand immediate attention. Or it may be a time when we feel that we must maintain the morale of others so that we do not initially react to or feel the loss. Our own grief is delayed as we take care of business or other people, rather than attending to and flowing with our feelings. These delayed reactions may be brief or may span a number of years. An example of a brief delayed reaction is depicted in the following story.

> A girl of sixteen lost both her parents and boyfriend in the [Coconut Grove] fire, and was herself severely burned with marked involvement of the lungs. Throughout her stay in the hospital, her attitude was that of cheerful acceptance without any sign of adequate distress. When she was discharged at the end of three weeks, she appeared cheerful, talked rapidly with considerable flow of ideas, seemed eager to return home and to assume the role of parent for her two younger siblings. Except for slight feelings of "lonesomeness," she complained of no distress. This period of griefless acceptance continued for the next two months, even when the household was dispersed and her younger siblings were placed in other homes. Not until the end of the tenth week did she begin to show a true state of grief with marked feelings of depression, intestinal emptiness, tightness in her throat, frequent crying and vivid preoccupation with her deceased parents.[2]

In cases where the grief is delayed for years, it can be triggered anew by an event in the present which brings about memories of circumstances surrounding the loss. One circumstance which reactivates memories of the loss is when the bereaved individual reaches the age that the lost loved one was when she or he died. This is seen when an individual who loses a parent attempts to bury the grief reaction to this loss. The grief may be kept successfully at bay for many years, but as the person nears the age the lost parent was at the time of death, memories of that person resurface. Along with these memories come the feelings of grief that have been stored away. Lindemann observed this peculiar circumstance in the case of a railroad worker who sought treatment at the clinic. He was experiencing a deep grief reaction for which he had no explanation. He was forty-two years old. Investigation uncovered the fact that his mother had committed suicide when she was forty-two years old. His delayed grief over this loss surfaced as he reached the age that his mother had been at the time of her death.

If our grief is delayed for a long time or if the grief has been totally denied, our behavior will take on extreme changes. This is a distorted grief reaction.

## Distorted Grief Reaction

Some of the changes in behavior that Lindemann saw as distorted grief were:

1. restless activity without a feeling of loss
2. psychosomatic diseases such as colitis, arthritis, and asthma

3. physical symptoms that are the same as or similar to those of the last illness of the deceased
4. changes in relationships with friends and relatives, with signs of withdrawal and isolation
5. furious rage targeted toward specific persons such as the doctors who treated the lost loved one
6. "flat affect," where the person apparently has no feelings because he or she has masked angry, hostile feelings
7. indecision, lack of initiative, and the loss of social skills
8. engagement in behavior that may be harmful to the person's social and economic existence (such as giving away necessary belongings)
9. highly agitated depression with extreme anxiety, low self-esteem, guilt, and an expressed need for punishment. Those who show these particular behavior patterns are seen as dangerously suicidal.[3]

We experience some of these symptoms during normal grief, so how do we know if our grief is really distorted? When these changes in our behavior are exaggerated and their duration is prolonged, that can indicate distortions of normal grief.

The grief-blocking mire can be a result of unresolved grief which takes on the forms of delayed and distorted reactions. Delayed reactions lead to distorted reactions which cause extreme behavior changes. How is it that unresolved grief can cause such dangerous changes in normal behavior? When the flow of our feelings is stopped, our movement through the process of grief comes to a halt. Our unfolding ceases. Distorted grief reactions may be the result of being stuck, at a complete standstill in one of the stages of our process of grief.

Parkes, in his model of the grief process, implies that each stage of the process carries with it a specific task.[4] Each task must be completed before the person can move into the next phase and begin dealing with the next issue in movement toward final resolution.

The task of the shock stage seems to be to cushion the impact of the loss, to lessen its reality for a while until the body is able and ready to begin to experience the real impact of the loss. In the searching/pining phase, we search for and find in some way what was lost and then internalize or take it into ourselves. The task of the depression stage seems to lie in the painful work of letting go of, or releasing, the internalized loss. Restructuring is centered around reorganizing the disrupted lifespace caused by the loss.

If the task inherent in each stage is not finished, then the possibility exists that we can remain in that specific stage, remaining fixed in its pain and distress. We become blocked and the energy, the charge of our feelings that tied us to our loss, is not freed or redirected. It becomes snarled and knotted, and as a result movement through the process is thwarted; this causes disruptions in the normal patterns of our behavior. John Bowlby recognized the possibility of getting stuck in the mire of grief:

> Bowlby maintains, however, that an individual can become fixated at any point in the process: he can continue to reject the fact of death (or any type of loss), he can remain disorganized, torn by intense emotions, or he can reach a stalemate in an early stage of reorganization that is insufficient for his effective response to the demands of living.[5]

Thus we see that if we allow long delays in flowing with the feelings of grief, this may lead to grief distortions. If we don't finish with the task of a particular stage, the distortions in our behavior that appear may be manifestations of our being lodged in one of the stages of the grief process. This lack of movement may then interfere with the normal functioning of daily life. The difference in our behavior is then noticed by friends and relatives.

Within Parkes' model of grief there are two places where we are most likely to get stuck: in the searching/pining and depression stages. The shock stage serves as our brief delay from dealing with the reality of loss; eventually, shock passes, and the reality of the loss is experienced. So it is unlikely that we would become immobilized in this stage. The restructuring phase unfolds *after* we have accepted the reality and permanence of the loss and have released it. So becoming trapped in this stage is also unlikely.

If we delay our grief and stop the flow of our feelings, our movement through the process is halted. Long delays of the flow can lead to distorted grief reactions. If we stop the flow of our feelings of grief, we may get stuck in the mire.

We've seen what flow is, why it is important, and the consequences of stopping the flow of our feelings of grief.

Now we will explore in more detail the effects of being stuck in the mire, and will provide tools for pulling ourselves out. First, we will look at the consequences and dangers of being stuck in the mire. Then we will follow the process of grief and see the forms it takes in a person's life as the flow is disturbed. We'll also look at factors that contribute to becoming trapped in the mire. Finally, we will learn how to tell if we're stuck, find ways of allowing ourselves to get moving again, explore ways to avoid the mire altogether, and see how we might create flow, the third ingredient in our formula for living with loss.

The glaring neon light flashed on the dingy curtain in Darlene's living room. Alone in the dark, she stared at the never-changing designs. It seemed as though they were continuously reminding her of where she was. The loud, drunken voices and the blaring music from the outdated juke box drifted in from the seedy bar across the street. For a moment she caught the musty odor of stale beer and cigarettes. The ice cubes in her drink rattled noisily against the glass as she pushed it toward her lips. She took a deep drag on her cigarette and was distracted by the contrast of the fiery glow of the lit ash against the still black night. Darlene had never lived downtown before. She'd always considered it a lonely, scary area—a place where losers and broken-down winos lived. Her tiny, rickety apartment surrounded by concrete, bars, and five-and-dime stores was far away from the quiet tree-lined streets where she'd always lived. But it was all right, she kept telling herself; everything was okay. She didn't care because nothing mattered any more, nothing at all.

Within the flow of the process of grief there is natural movement. But when the flow becomes disturbed, delayed, or stopped, the movement of grief is altered and the mire—thick, dark, heavy mud surrounded by a sullen haze—begins to form. Its thickness oozes around our legs, weighing them down as it pulls us deeper. It makes us weary; each step becomes harder to take. And after a while we become stuck, unable to move. Being immobilized with grief brings particular dangers to our health and well-being. In this chapter we'll examine the hazards of being stuck in the mire.

## THE DANGERS OF BEING STUCK IN THE MIRE

Trapped in the mire, our movement through grief is blocked. We are stranded, stuck in a particular phase, ruminating on the stagnant feelings of that place—not freeing them, not working them through. When the flow of grief is stopped, the energy that was tied to our loss is not let go. It becomes dammed up deep inside. Roadblocks stop its natural tendency to move toward wholeness and healing. Since grief can't move down its normal path, it may turn toward other, more dangerous roads. The energy changes and takes on different forms. It can bring changes into our lives in three major areas: physical, emotional, and behavioral.

### Physical Changes

When unresolved grief begins to move down more dangerous pathways, having been blocked by mire, this can show itself in the form of illness, disease, or even death. Lindemann, as we discussed in the last chapter, saw these changes as distorted grief reactions that manifest themselves in physical symptoms similar to those occurring in the last illness of the lost loved one, and in psychosomatic diseases like colitis, arthritis, and asthma. Stone, in *Suicide and Grief,* perceives a connection between being stuck in unresolved grief and physical illness:

> Some of these people who have physical symptoms of distress have stopped at one of the stages. Unless someone can help them work through the emotional problems involved in the stage at which they seem fixed, they will remain ill.[6]

Elisabeth Kübler-Ross, in her book *On Death and Dying,* interviewed people who were ill and many who were dying. A portion of her interview with Mr. E. illustrates the way in which we can become ill as a result of being stalled in our mourning:

> Mr. E., an eighty-year-old Jewish man, was admitted to the medical service of a private hospital because of severe weight loss, anorexia, and constipation. He complained of unbearable abdominal pains and looked haggard and tired. His general mood was depressed and he wept easily ... He

related how he had been well until four months before admission, when he suddenly became "an old sick and lonely man." Further questioning revealed that a few weeks before the onset of all his physical complaints he had lost a daughter-in-law, and two weeks before the onset of his pains, his estranged wife died suddenly while he was on vacation and out of town.[7]

According to Kübler-Ross, Mr. E. gradually came face to face with his feelings about his losses and worked them through to resolution. With this, his physical symptoms cleared up completely. But what if we do not deal with the feelings or issues that are keeping us stuck in our grief? It is possible that these illnesses may progress into a disease state. Two diseases in which there has been some research indicating a link between loss and disease are cancer and rheumatoid arthritis.

### Cancer

Cancer research shows that each of us carries the potential for cancer. But why does cancer remain dormant in some people and not in others? And what is the nature of the body's defense reaction to cancer? Why does the body's natural defense against cancer hold up in some people and not in others? It may be that emotional stresses are somehow translated to a biochemical level which in some way alters the body's defense against cancer.

A theory that attempts to explain the dynamics of emotional stress and its transformation to a biochemical disruption of the body's immune system has been formulated and presented by Simonton and his associates. They have proposed a model which suggests that physical and psychological states may interact upon each other in setting the stage for the onset of cancer.[8] The theory demonstrates the way in which psychological stress leads to depression and despair and how these mind states can affect the body in a kind of chain reaction. According to these researchers, destructive psychological states of depression and despair can react on the body through the limbic system, which in turn affects hypothalamus activity. Hypothalamus activity regulates the immune system; when it is disrupted, the result is ultimately a disturbance in the endocrine system functioning. All of these links in the chain, when affected by negative mind states, can pave the way for the development of cancer. Let's look at this theory in further detail.

*Psychological stress,* particularly stress created by traumatic loss, has been shown to occur prior to the onset of cancer. According to Simonton and his associates,

> Both the research and our own observations of patients indicate that major stresses are often a precursor to cancer. Frequently clusters of stresses occur within a short period of time. The critical stresses we have identified are those that threaten personal identity. These may include the death of a spouse or loved one, retirement, the loss of a significant role.[9]

Earlier we saw how major losses can be experienced as tremendous upheaval and as a result may present a threat to psychological balance. Traumatic loss disrupts our lifespace and creates an imbalance that can be experienced as a threat to our very survival. This threat rests on the way in which we deal with the stress. Predisposition to a disease such as cancer is not based solely on stress, but also on the way we cope with stress. If we can find no way to deal with the stress, then we begin to feel trapped. When we can't find a way out of the box of *depression* and *despair,* we end up feeling hopeless and helpless. These feelings can lead to a sense of giving up on life. A life-threatening disease can become a way out:

> Once there is no hope, then the individual is just "running in place," never expecting to go anywhere. On the surface he or she may seem to be coping with life, but internally, life seems to hold no further meaning except in maintaining conventions. Serious illness or death represents a solution, an exit, or a postponement of the problem.[10]

The *limbic system* of the body acts as kind of a computer which stores up stress, feelings, and sensations of the body. The feelings of being trapped within depression and despair, the feelings of hopelessness and helplessness, the sense of giving up, all are "stored" in the computer of the limbic system. All of these feelings are then sent from the limbic system to the hypothalamus.

The *hypothalamus* is a tiny spot in the brain that regulates the immune system and the activity of the pituitary gland:

> The messages the hypothalamus receives from the limbic system are then translated in two important ways: First, part of the hypothalamus—that part most responsive to human stress—participates in controlling the immune system. Second, the hypothalamus plays a critical role in regulating the activity of the pituitary gland which in turn regulates the remainder of the endocrine system with its vast range of hormonal control functions throughout the body.[11]

The body's natural defense is its *immune system,* whose function is to fight off and destroy alien and harmful cell growth. The stress from the feelings of depression, despair, hopelessness and helplessness, and the sense of giving up are relayed through the limbic system to the hypothalamus. This stress may cause the hypothalamus to foul up the workings of the immune system:

> In this mind/body model, emotional stress, mediated by the limbic system via the hypothalamus, produces a suppression of the immune system which leaves the body susceptible to the development of cancer.[12]

The hypothalamus is the director of the *pituitary gland* which in turn directs the *endocrine system*. The stressed hypothalamus receives messages of severe, prolonged depression and despair and triggers the pituitary gland, which throws the switch on the endocrine system in such a way that the body changes:

> To complicate matters, evidence suggests that the hypothalamus, responding to stress, triggers the pituitary gland in such a way that the hormonal balance of the body—mediated by the endocrine system—is changed. This is particularly significant since an imbalance in adrenal hormones has been shown to create a greater susceptibility to carcinogenic substances.[13]

With the creation of the hormonal imbalance there exists the possibility of "the production of abnormal cells in the body and a weakening ability of the immune system to combat these cells."[14] And with this, the scene has been set for the growth of cancerous cells. That is the way in which emotional stress (mind) may be effecting physiology (body) in the development of cancer.

Loss has been shown to be a type of stress that precedes cancer. The work of Simonton and his associates with patients who have cancer demonstrates this pattern over and over again:

> Betty Johnson, a forty-year-old woman, came to the hospital with an advanced cancer of the kidney. She had been widowed during the preceding year but continued to live and work on the ranch left to her by her husband. An exploratory operation revealed that she had cancer that had spread outside the kidney and that it would be impossible to remove the cancer surgically. She was treated with minimal doses of radiation, but there was little expectation for improvement. Then she was sent home to her ranch given only a few months to live. Once home, she fell in love with one of the men who worked on her ranch and they were soon married. Despite the prognosis of imminent death, she showed no further signs of illness for five years. Then her second husband left her after running through her money. Within a few weeks, Betty had a major occurrence of the cancer and died shortly thereafter.[15]

All of us at different times in our lives experience loss. Some of us may develop cancer after traumatic loss, while others may not. Why does the body's defense system hold up in some of us and not others? The link between loss and cancer may be found in unresolved grief. When the stress of grief is blocked, it may stay within the body and gradually, as seen in Simonton's model, affect the body in the development of cancer.

In the 1800s, a New York surgeon, Willard Parker, worked with breast cancer patients. He believed that grief was tied to patients who developed diseases such as cancer.

There are the strongest physiological reasons for believing that great mental depression, particularly grief, induces a predisposition to such disease as cancer or becomes the exciting cause under circumstances where the predisposition has already been acquired.[16]

R. W. Bathrop and his associates also concluded that grief affects the body's immune system, thus possibly causing cancer:

> Dr. R. W. Bathrop and his associates at the University of New South Wales, Australia, have conducted studies indicating that bereavement lowers the body's immune system. They tested twenty-six bereaved persons at two weeks and six weeks after their spouses' deaths. A control group was established of twenty-six hospital employees who had not experienced any bereavement in the past two years. Lymphocite function, a critical measure of the potency of the body's immune system, was significantly depressed in those who had lost a wife or husband. Since the immune system serves as a potent defense against the reproduction of cancerous cells ... evidence that emotional loss can lead to a suppression of the immune system is an important clue to the cause of cancer.[17]

Unresolved grief that is created when a person becomes stuck in the mire of the depression stage may be the dynamic of how loss can lead to cancer. If movement through the process of grief stops because we are unable or unwilling to let go of the loss, we can become stranded at this stage. In order to understand this better, let's take a closer look at the issues that must be resolved at this stage so that we can move on.

It is at this stage that the permanence of the loss is realized and attempts to get it back are abandoned. The realization that the person (or object) who was lost is never coming back leads to the feelings of despair, depression, and apathy. The main issue of this phase is the *acceptance* of the permanence of the loss and the gradual letting go of it. If we refuse to accept the loss and relinquish it, then we remain stalled in this stage, with a heightening of the feelings of despair and depression. Prolonged depression can lead to a sense of being dead inside, with life no longer having meaning. A person who is trapped inside this box may eventually lose the desire to live. The self-destructive attitude of wanting to die, giving up, could be transmitted biochemically so the natural body defenses are suppressed, the body changes, and the stage is set for the onset of cancer.

> It is the giving up on life that plays a role in interfering with the immune system and may, through changes in the hormonal balance, lead to an increase in the production of abnormal cells. Physically it creates the climate that is right for the development of cancer.[18]

Anger and guilt are two very intense emotions experienced in the depression stage. If these feelings are not vented and released, if we hold onto these feelings, we become stuck at this stage of grief. This relates to the development of cancer in a very interesting way. Cancer researchers have postulated typical personality characteristics of patients with malignancies. Goldfarb, Drieson, and Cole have theorized that two personality traits that are applicable to unresolved grief are the inability to express anger and the inability to accept the loss of a valued other.[19] The main task of the depression stage of grief is the acceptance of the loss and its subsequent *release*. In order for this to happen, the feelings of anger and guilt have to be resolved. Those who do not resolve these issues and feelings will remain in this phase. It seems likely that people with the personality characteristics cited by Goldfarb and his associates are likely to get stuck in the third stage of grief.

Cancer researchers have noticed a link between feelings of helplessness and despair prior to the onset of a malignancy. The inability to work through the issues and feelings of this phase will magnify the feelings that are already present. With the perception that there is no way out of the despair, it doesn't seem hard to postulate a connection of unresolved grief and cancer.

> Sammuel T. Kowell, of Boston University, has investigated the attitudes of eighteenth and nineteenth century physicians toward cancer. According to Kowell's overview . . . these physicians were impressed by the frequency with which certain life situations seemed to occur prior to the development of neoplasm or cancerous growth. A common denominator which they noted was a reaction of despair and hopelessness following such diverse occurrences as the death of a friend or relative, separation, economic, political, professional and other frustrations. These patients apparently lost all desire to live and by virtue of this type of passive surrender, the stage was set for the development of a malignancy.[20]

This type of depression, labeled "reactive depression," and the feelings of depression experienced in the third stage of grief are the same phenomenon. The expression of the feelings of despair, apathy, anger, and guilt that make up this phase are very important. If they are shunned and buried rather than brought out into the sunlight and openly expressed and experienced, they can take the dark direction toward illness and disease.

If anger is not expressed outwardly, it will seek inward expression and will be felt as guilt. Where there is guilt there is the need for self-punishment. Acquiring a fatal disease or catastrophic illness is a form of punishment of the self. Development of a fatal disease means death. Death is the final way out of the intense emotions that are churned up as a result of being stuck in the mire. A fatal illness such as cancer may be a means of resolving grief, a way of ending the pain and suffering of the depression stage without moving through it.

### Rheumatoid Arthritis

In research on rheumatoid arthritis, psychic disequilibrium was cited as a possible cause of the disease. As we have seen, the lifespace of the individual is severely disrupted by major loss and the circle of the person's life is thrown off-balance. Loss does create psychic disequilibrium. Grief is the process by which equilibrium is once more restored to the person's life. Remaining in the mire will magnify and increase the state of imbalance.

The inability to express anger was also noted as a personality trait of people who suffer from this disease. When anger is inhibited, guilt appears and again, the self-destructive forces within begin to emerge. With these two factors in mind, it is conceivable that being lodged in the depression stage, with the movement of grief blocked, could also take the form of rheumatoid disease. The self-destructive state of mind that is created by the mire could cause the body to self-destruct.

> Rheumatoid arthritis and osteoarthritis are classified, along with such diseases as ulcerative colitis, as autoimmune diseases. Since these disorders literally involve the body's "turning on itself," researchers have wondered whether a particular form of self-destructive personality might not translate into an autoimmune and neurophysiological self-destructiveness.[21]

Not only can being stuck in the mire lead to illness and diseases like cancer and rheumatoid arthritis, it can also lead to death.

People do die who have suffered a loss. It may be the overwhelming pain of the loss caused by unresolved grief that is killing them. Evidence of this can be seen in studies on widowhood. In 1963 Young, Benjamin, and Wallis studied the shock of widowhood and the mortality rate that followed.[22] They used a sample of 4,486 widowers fifty-five years and older, half of whose wives had died in January 1957 and the other half whose wives had died in July 1957. Each subject was followed up for five years. There was an increase in the mortality rates among the widowed population, with the peak of mortality occurring during the first year of bereavement. Forty percent of the widowers died within the first six months of bereavement. Young and associates commented on the causes of these deaths:

> ... in widowed people ... tuberculosis of the respiratory system, syphillis, cancer, diabetes, iron deficiency, anemia, vascular lesions of the central nervous system, degenerative and hypertensive heart disease, cirrhosis of the liver, diseases of the pancreas, and suicide are particularly responsible for the higher mortality rate of the widowed as compared with the married.[23]

Not allowing the flow of grief can also cause death, as seen in the following excerpt:

> This man in his forties and in good health had tenderly and devotedly nursed his dying wife. Immediately after her death, he plunged into work, moved, got busy with arrangements for himself and his children, intent on keeping a stiff upper lip and denying any needs of his own. He became angry and upset with his children who showed clear signs of disturbances after their mother's death. He was not only unable to help them, but alienated them as much as possible. Six months after his wife's death, this man contracted a terminal illness and died.[24]

The physical forms that unresolved grief may take can eventually prove fatal. Destroying ourselves through fatal illnesses may be an unconscious way of attempting to relieve and resolve the pain of unresolved grief.

## Emotional Changes

Changes in our emotional state due to being trapped in the mire may appear in the guises of anxiety and fear, depression, and emotional breakdowns.

### Anxiety and Fear

As a result of the unresolved grief from my grandfather's death, I spent many years struggling with the anxiety and fears that seemed to come out of nowhere. When he suffered the heart attack I was six years old. My main memory of his death was hearing his final breaths escaping from his body. To me it had sounded as though he were choking. I carried the grief from his death for many years and developed a fear of choking to death. Swallowing pills was an impossibility for me and later, in my adolescent years, I became tense and would choke on any stringy food when I found myself in an unfamiliar social setting that aroused anxiety. Now I understand that my choking phobia was really an attempt to choke back the feelings of unresolved grief from this loss.

My sister Marj discovered the body of a friend who had had a kidney problem and died from alcohol poisoning. This traumatic loss aroused intense feelings of anxiety and fear which plagued her for about six months. During that time she developed a fear of the dark and slept with the light on.

Anxiety and fear are smokescreens for deeper feelings like anger, guilt, and sorrow. When we keep a lid on the deeper feelings, our anxiety and fear mount, causing more distress, suffering, and conflict. Whenever any feeling is buried it becomes bigger, and new anxieties arise. In order to maintain a sense of control, we attempt to subdue these newer feelings of distress, suffering, and conflict as well. And continued suppression of feelings can lead to depression.

*Depression*

Depression is a low place. It is a place where we press our feelings down because we don't want to feel them.

> The act of depressing serves to keep the feelings from tearing one apart with rage, grief, and hopeless despair. This is what a depression is mostly about. It actually serves a useful purpose in subduing the pain and suffering of conflict.[25]

In normal grieving, we pass through the depression stage, experiencing the grief feelings in our own time. As we slowly resolve the issues of this phase, the depression lifts. But movement through this phase can be halted when the feelings are banished, totally cut off from our experience. The mourning, the working through, stops. At this point we become embedded in a deeper depression. All the energy that had been used for doing the work of grieving is now being used to continually stuff those feelings down, away from our experience. Life feels weary and tiresome.

An inability to feel and express the emotions of anger and guilt can lead to a heightening of the already existing depression. The suppression of our anger and guilt feelings may keep us tied to this depression stage of grief. The following story illustrates how burying her guilt kept one woman in the third stage and surrounded her life with the fog of severe depression:

> . . . [Mrs. Draper's] husband owned a furniture store. Their son-in-law, their only daughter's husband, was his partner. He was an efficient young man, but found it difficult to stand up to his father-in-law and this lack of cooperation was detrimental to the business. There were considerable debts and many worries for which Mrs. Draper blamed her husband. After his death, however, she blamed herself, feeling that her nagging may have contributed to the heart trouble which killed him. To make up for having been so hard on her husband while he was alive, she entered the business immediately after his death and made it her full-time concern. There was no time for mourning. A year later, Mrs. Draper asked for therapeutic help because of bouts of depression. She had become increasingly unable to enjoy the success of her business, feeling uneasy about succeeding where her husband had failed. Her guilt and depression could be seen as aspects of a delayed mourning process.[26]

Mrs. Draper's mourning process was halted as she pushed away from the feelings of guilt concerning her husband's death. She was entrenched in the depression stage; thus her grief was unresolved and she became extremely depressed.

Kübler-Ross tells of a cancer patient who was immobilized in this phase of grief, not because of his illness, but due to unresolved grief:

> He was not thinking of his cancer as much as he was reviewing the meaning of his life and searching for ways to share this with the most significant person—his wife. He was deeply depressed, not because of his terminal illness, but because he had not finished his own mourning for [his] dead parents and child.[27]

Depression is an attempt to avoid the intense feelings of guilt and anger. In depression, feelings are pushed away. If we stay in that place, we eventually end up feeling nothing. To feel nothing is to experience a death within ourselves; "The move toward depression is a move toward deadness."[28]

### Emotional Breakdown

Prolonged depression can lead to emotional breakdowns. As we continue to suppress feelings, they seem to grow out of proportion. Trying to maintain a sense of control through the denial of feelings can lead to a total loss of control. When we attempt to master and control feelings instead of flowing with them and experiencing them, we can end up being controlled by the very feelings that we fought so desperately to control. This loss of control is known to lay people as an emotional breakdown. Here the motion of our feelings break down. They splinter and shatter, flying in a million directions. The result is confusion, disorientation, and a sense of imbalance. Our behavior is beyond our control, erratic, irrational. Everything in our lifespace is out of sync. Our minds, bodies, feelings have all split apart. They no longer work together as a unit.

In the story of Mrs. Leather, we can see an example of this. Mrs. Leather had been widowed when her husband died of a brain tumor. She was twenty-eight years old when she suffered this loss. With five children to raise alone, she did not give herself the time to fully mourn her loss. After many years, her children married and had families of their own. When her youngest son lost his wife through divorce, his children were placed in her care. She nurtured them for many years. When she was seventy, her eldest son took the children into his home to provide for them. World War II was raging at this time, and losing her grandchildren set off a war within her.

> She never said what it meant to her, but it must have meant a great deal because a few months later she had what was called a nervous breakdown and was admitted to the hospital. Her sons were given leave when they found, with horror, their mother's apartment full of rats and mice. For many weeks she had not eaten her rations but had hoarded them in the cupboard where they went bad. She was very confused when they visited her in the hospital and insisted that God had forbidden her to eat. After a life of caring for others, Mrs. Leather saw no purpose in caring for herself now that she had no one else to care for.[29]

Mrs. Leather was out of control. Her mind, body, and feelings had all split apart and the movement of her feelings broke down.

Without movement through the depression stage, the feelings magnify and the urgent need to push them down becomes paramount. The more we cut off feelings, the more dead we become inside. This feeling state leads us to a life that is devoid of meaning and a path filled with self-destruction. This self-destructive mind state, caused by unfinished grief, can manifest itself in physical, emotional, and behavioral forms. Taking the physical road, it can lead to illness, disease, and even death. If it takes the emotional route, it can lead to severe depression and emotional breakdown. In the following section we will look at some of the behavioral changes that can come about when one is stuck in the mire.

## Behavioral Changes

Some of the behavioral changes brought about from unresolved grief involve self-destructive behaviors such as substance abuse and suicide.

### Substance Abuse

Substance abuse refers to the misuse of substances like alcohol and drugs. Being mired in grief means continuously carrying around the horrendous pain and emotions of loss. Since the feelings are plugged, since they are being neither felt or expressed, they are not lessening or being released. One way of coping with the intensity of being stuck is to sedate the body and mind with alcohol or drugs to attain temporary relief.

> ... alcohol actually has a depressant effect on the nervous system. That is actually one of its effects. By depressing those impulses which reach consciousness, and make one feel tense, anxious and self-critical, alcohol serves to inhibit recognition of those feelings. By diminishing normal neurological integrity in that fashion—that is, by interfering with the messages that reach the mind, alcohol seems to offer relief from anxiety, shyness, and depression.[30]

Alcohol temporarily masks the feeling of grief. Then another bout of depression occurs, induced by the toxic effect of the alcohol. More alcohol is consumed to hide that depression, and the cycle of addiction begins. "So continual drinking then serves as a form of anesthesia in a futile attempt to deal with mounting anxiety and depression."[31]

Alcoholism can be seen as a means of trying to lock away the feeling aroused by being caught in the mire of grief. It is a way of dulling the sharp feelings of rage, guilt, despair, and sorrow. Addiction to any drug can serve a similar purpose.

Loss brings in its wake the tremendous pain and stress of grief. This stress, if carried for an indefinite time, can become overwhelming to one's mind and body. Alcohol and drugs can be a means of escape from that stress. Drug addiction and alcoholism are escape hatches that we use to keep us from confronting the feelings that pile up as movement through grief stops. Bringing the flow of grief to a halt can lead to changes in behavior that grow into addictions. Dorpat cites an example of this type of behavioral change:

> Depression of grief affects and denial of the meaning of his father's suicide characterized the responses of a young physician first treated in office psychotherapy and then hospitalized for alcoholism. When he was fifteen he had found his father dead from a shotgun blast. With the tacit encouragement of his mother, he immediately assumed the management of the home. Moments after he found his dead father he ordered the servants to serve dinner and to proceed as if the suicide had never occurred. Both denied the loss and their feelings of rage, guilt, and abandonment over the suicide. Within a year the mother began a lengthy hospitalization for treatment of alcoholism and suicidal depression. Later the patient became depressed and he, too, attempted to relieve the depression by consuming ever-increasing quantities of alcohol.[32]

Stagnating in the depression phase of grief over his father's suicide, this young doctor tried to mask the intense feelings by consuming more and more alcohol. As a result he became increasingly depressed, drank more to hide that depression, and finally became addicted to alcohol. His major disturbance, the unresolved grief, became compounded by the added problem of alcoholism.

### Suicide

The ultimate self-destructive behavior resulting from being stuck in the mire is suicide. To understand the way in which suicide can become a way out of the mire, a means for resolving grief, we need to examine the two stages in which suicidal ideation is present. These are the searching/pining and depression stages.

The searching/pining stage has two facets—that of searching and finding. The main issue to be resolved here is to recover whatever has been lost. The searching behavior is in no way aimless. According to Parkes, in terms of a death loss, it has the specific purpose of finding the one who was lost.[33] The primary means for finding the lost loved one is by "internalizing" him or her. We search and in some way we find. Then we take the loss and make it a part of us. This alleviates some of the pain of grief.

The psyche, injured by acute grief, seems to make the experience tolerable by a situational response called "identification" or sometimes "incorporation." The bereaved person seeks to overcome the pain of grief by becoming one with the lost object.[34]

Another way of becoming one with the lost person is by joining the loved one in death. This is one way of finding the person. Stone, in his study of bereaved widows, noted that several of the women had toyed with the idea of suicide as a means for rejoining the lost person in death:

> One widow stated, "I felt like killing myself when my mother died. Only the love and support of my husband saw me through that unhappy time. I believe if it had not been for my children I would have taken my own life when my husband died. I had a very strong urge to join him."[35]

Parkes concluded that human adults must go through the motions of searching and finding in order to begin to untie the attachment to the loss and move on with the work of grief.[36] Since suicidal ideation and impulses are features of this stage, the person who is blocked here and cannot alleviate some of the pain by internalizing the loss into the self may come to see suicide as a way of both relieving the pain and finding the lost loved one. Remaining stuck in this stage could cause a person to become dangerously suicidal.

An examination of the depression stage reveals that the major task here is the painful disengagement from the internalized loss. If we are to successfully work through this phase, we must accept the permanence of our loss. What was lost will never return. Our lives will never be the same. At this point, our searching and finding has to come to an end. In accepting that our loss is permanent, we stop trying to recover it and begin to work on releasing it. If our loss is not released, disturbances may occur. Anderson studied 100 patients between the years 1944 and 1947 who were under his care for disturbed grief reactions.[37] He described severe depression in which the individuals felt that they had no right to live while their loved ones were dead. They reasoned that their transgressions had caused the loved ones to die. Why else would their loved ones have gone away and left them? In their minds they had permanently lost someone very valuable because of conscious and unconscious, real and imagined, aggression toward that person. It was too late to make amends. This guilt and despair tied them to their lost loved ones. They could not release the lost loved ones and believed that the only way to make amends was to die, also. Suicide was a way of achieving this end. The grieving people carried within themselves images and memories of their lost loved one. Despair set in as they realized they had lost someone of great value who had played a significant role in their lives.

The despair seemed to be related to the fact that it was too late to make amends. Depression emerged as the emotional reaction to this realization. Holding on to this made it impossible to let go of the lost person.

In the natural process of our grief we can experience the same type of feelings, but as the loss is accepted and released, the depression lifts. Severe depression, caused by the failure to deal with and free guilt and anger, can lead us to a place where we feel that we must die also. This then feeds into the already existing suicidal impulses that are inherent at this stage. Long periods of constant depression when one is stuck here can cause already-present suicidal thoughts and impulses to become stronger.

One of the distorted reactions recorded by Lindemann was that of agitated depression where the bereaved person became dangerously suicidal. Lindemann saw this behavior as being a manifestation of unresolved grief. It may be that the unresolved feelings and issues of the depression stage can cause this behavior.

A young man, aged thirty-two, had received only minor burns [from the Coconut Grove fire] and left the hospital apparently well on the road to recovery just before the psychiatric survey [psychiatric interviews] of disaster victims [survivors of the disastrous fire] took place. On the fifth day he had learned that his wife had died. He seemed somewhat relieved of his worry about her fate; he impressed the surgeon as being unusually well-controlled during the following short period of his stay in the hospital. On January 1st he was returned to the hospital by his family. Shortly after his return home he had become restless, did not want to stay at home, had taken a trip to see relatives trying to find some rest, had not succeeded, and had returned home in a state of marked agitation, appearing preoccupied, frightened, and unable to concentrate on any organized activity. The mental status presented a somewhat unusual picture. He was restless, could not sit still or participate in any activity on the ward . . . He complained about his feeling of extreme tension, an inability to breathe, generalized weakness and exhaustion, and his frantic fear that something terrible was going to happen . . . With intense morbid guilt feelings, he reviewed incessantly the events of the fire. His wife had stayed behind. When he tried to pull her out he had fainted and was shoved out by the crowd. She was burned while he was saved . . . He complained about being filled with incredible violence and did not know what to do about it. He slept poorly with large sedation . . . In the course of four days he became somewhat more composed, had longer periods of contact with the psychiatrist, and seemed to feel that he was being understood and might be able to cope with his morbid feelings of guilt and violent impulses. On the sixth day, of his hospital stay, however, after skillfully distracting the attention of his special nurse, he jumped through a closed window to a violent death.[38]

This man was immobilized by feelings of guilt, abandonment, and rage. As these feelings take on greater proportions because they have not been resolved, suicide can become a way out, a way of relieving the hopeless feelings of despair, and a way of resolving the loss without accepting its permanence and relinquishing it. Being stuck in the depression stage can lead people toward the act of taking their own lives.

Remaining stuck in the mire brings with it many dangers. The physical dangers are illness, disease, and even death. Emotionally, the dangers are anxiety and fears, depression and breakdowns. Self-destructive behaviors of substance abuse and suicide are some of the behavioral dangers. So it is readily apparent that the unresolved grief from blocking the flow of grief can become life-threatening.

In the next section we will follow two people through their processes of grief and see how their lives changed as they became immobilized. We'll also explore what causes us to get stuck.

The bare light bulb cast a hard, dark shadow on the yellowed, aging tiles in the bathroom. The sink, ringed with a light brown film, stood blemished with spots of dried soap left from weeks of neglect. Darlene jumped, startled from her sleep as another faceless man slammed the door on her. In the faint light of dawn, she dragged herself into the bathroom to pour soothing streams of cold water over her bruises. Making love was supposed to be gentle. For her it had been brutal. But it didn't matter. She was numb to the pain. She didn't care. Catching her reflection in the glaring light of the mirror, a wave of disgust and self-loathing washed over her. There was no recognition of the person staring back. "Who are you? Why are you doing this? I hate you!" she screamed.

While the storm rages on, stalled overhead, the mire becomes deeper and thicker, preventing all movement. As the motion of the storm of grief stops, the mire traps us, sucking us deeper and deeper, causing our lives to take on weird distortions. As we move through this section, we will follow the storms of two people as they became entrenched in the mire and see the dangerous directions that their lives took through their immobilization. We'll also discover additional factors that can trap us in the mire.

## MARJI'S STORM

Marji, a thirty-eight-year-old single parent of four, worked in the mental health field. In December she had lost her grandfather, with whom she'd been very close. He had died the day after Christmas and his death shocked her because it was totally unexpected. She didn't mourn her loss, and put her feelings on a shelf because she had other very pressing matters to deal with at that time. So her grief from this major loss was buried until March, when she experienced a cluster of losses and another shattering death.

It was early in the morning and the newscaster on the radio promised a sunny and fair day. A little tired from the week's work, Marji was relieved that it was finally Friday. She sauntered into a colleague's office just as she was hanging up the phone. Betty handed her the newspaper and pointed at the article. There in large, bold print, it said that David was dead. Not comprehending, she read the first sentence that spelled it out in black and white; he had attempted to kill his wife and then had killed himself. She collapsed into the chair as her knees gave way. Tears poured down her face and her chest heaved with deep sobs. Betty, unaware that Marji and David had been close friends or that she had talked with him the previous week, rushed over and held her. Marji felt totally undone. Through her tears she saw clouds gathering outside the window.

As the grief from one loss is pushed down, it is stored away. When loss strikes again, all of these buried feelings are unearthed. So we end up being barraged by former grief as well as by the present feelings. Marji was overwhelmed as she was struck with piggyback losses and doubled feelings of grief. Not only did she have the devastation of David's suicide to deal with; she also had the horrendous pain and hurt from the loss of her beloved grandfather.

Marji's shock and numbness began immediately and extended into the next few weeks as the image of the newspaper continuously printed itself across her mind.

Her hand shook violently with another tremor and she dropped the pencil. A sense of weakness possessed her and she burst into tears, unable to control their flow. That was what scared her the most. She had no control over anything. Her tears seemed to finish as the flashing red light on the intercom called to her. Composed now, she pressed it. On line one was the accountant. Yes, she would take it. Answering the questions concerning the budget, Marji suddenly felt tears coming again. Immediately, she ended the call. Then another wave of tears was rushing over her.

Time became distorted. Marji couldn't eat or sleep. It seemed as though a part of her was standing outside of herself, refusing to believe that David had killed himself. She kept wondering when she was going to wake up from this nightmare, when this cruel joke would be over. How could it be true? The other part of her was very emotional and at times hysterical. She couldn't stop it. She felt split. Inside she felt crazy. On the outside she seemed like a zombie, unable to keep her thoughts away from David's death. At times she simply phased out. She just wasn't there, as her world took on a sense of the unreal.

After feeling some of the physical and psychological disturbances that are a part of shock, Marji began to move into the searching/pining stage.

Seated at her desk, the ledger open in front of her, Marji was lost in thought. If she could die, then she'd be able to see David. She'd know he was all right. But how was she going to die? She wasn't sick or anything. Maybe a car accident. She imagined the story on the 6 o'clock news describing her car as it had veered off the road and struck a tree. "What's wrong with me?" she thought, snapping herself back. Here she was, lost in fantasy about joining him in death by killing herself. Those thoughts frightened her, so she turned to the ledger. Adding up a column of numbers, she abruptly stopped, feeling the need to look for David. She played their final conversation back through her mind. It seemed as if that was all that she could concentrate on, every minute of every day. Everything else in her life had faded into the background. Maybe he wasn't really dead. A few times on the way home she'd gone by the restaurant he'd managed, and parked in her car, almost expecting to see him walk out the door. But he never came.

Marji's world was narrowing into preoccupation with her loss. Unable to concentrate, she was searching desperately for David. She eventually did find him.

The hair on the back of her neck stood up on end and a cold chill ran down her back. She was like a cat, arched and waiting. She had been telling herself to stay aware so that when he came she wouldn't miss him. He was here. She could feel him. His presence was in this room. It was as though he were not really gone. Marji had been sensing this presence from time to time during the last few weeks. It gave her a feeling of comfort. Feeling that he was still with her lessened the pain. She felt warm all over. David wasn't lost forever. He'd been found.

Marji's mire was formed in the depression phase of the storm. Feelings of guilt were jammed up inside her. The end of their flow stranded her in depression. She felt responsible for his death because she had failed to pick up his intent during their final phone conversation; Marji pinned the blame for his death on herself. She saw herself as solely responsible.

Survivors, the living friends and relatives of people who have killed themselves, are often plagued with overwhelming feelings of guilt and anger. Guilt is one of the primary feelings of the depression stage that must be worked through and released. When someone we love dies by his or her own hand, the guilt feelings take on monstrous proportions. The enormity of this guilt may lie in our feelings of anger and rage toward our lost one. We may feel angry because that person shut us out, dying rather than allowing us to help. We feel abandoned, left behind, blaming ourselves because we don't understand the why of it all.

Since it is difficult for us to justify our angry feelings toward someone hurt enough to commit suicide, our anger is not openly expressed and turns in the direction of guilt.

The bedroom was dark except for the moon highlighting the corners. Marji was away in her thoughts as she nervously snapped the telephone chord, striking the edge of the dresser again and again. The sense of guilt was heavy. And she beat herself with the "shoulds." She "should" have handled the situation better. She "should" have taken what he said about being down more seriously. She "should" have known he was crying for help when he called. She "should" have heard his intent underneath the words. After all, she was a mental health professional trained to listen to feelings, to hear subtle messages and cues. She "should" have known he was planning on death. She had blown it. There was no forgiveness for her because now he was dead. And his death lay heavy on her shoulders.

Marji could not let go of the guilt. She could not find room in her heart to forgive herself. And here her life energy began to take dangerous directions. When there is guilt and no movement toward its resolution and release, there is the need for punishment.

The alarm buzzed rudely in her ear. Another work day and she had no energy. As she dialed the number, taking yet another day off, she felt drained, burned out. She was no good at work anyway. Nothing was getting done. Bitterness welled up inside. Going to work was a chore that she just wasn't up to today. Besides, she had stopped caring about it weeks ago. The events at work no longer held any interest for her. When she was asked for input into a decision, she just sat there wishing the day was over so she could go home. She had nothing to say. There was nothing there that she wanted to deal with. No longer was she putting energy into her work. Apathy ruled.

One way that Marji punished herself was by sabotaging her job. Since she hadn't saved David, she didn't deserve to be working in this field. Losing her job, getting herself fired would be a punishment, atonement for her sins. So she stopped putting energy into it, hoping that eventually she'd be fired for not doing her work. The blocked grief was taking the form of emotional changes. She was falling into severe depression. Within these depths she was punishing herself through isolation from both her friends and her children.

The walls were closing in on her. She sat alone, cut off from the rest of the world. No longer reaching out to friends, afraid of being touched by their concern, she painstakingly built up the walls. She was careful about what she said to people, holding back key thoughts so they wouldn't know the depths of her depression. Withdrawing further, she was becoming walled off from her children as she realized that they had not been in her thoughts much over the past few months. She had not been dealing with them at all. Her time was no longer spent with them. Her time was spent in her bedroom, by herself, alone. Being responsible for David's death, she felt that she didn't deserve her children. She didn't deserve to live.

Marji also punished herself physically. Running every day had been a valuable part of her everyday routine. It made her feel good. She stopped running. Choosing to stay up late, she robbed herself of proper rest. Food no longer interested her. She either grabbed a bite of junk food or deliberately skipped meals. She didn't allow herself proper nutrition. Physically, she was running herself down. Emotionally, she was approaching the breaking point.

The sun was breaking through the clouds and she watched the dawning of a new day after another sleepless night. Now her awareness, like the sun, was breaking through. Hiding it all away was of no use now, she saw. In the dim light of the dawn it became so clear. Marji saw herself committing suicide. Like David, she was killing herself, only for her it was in a passive way. Her withdrawal and isolation and the abuse of her body were all part of that. She had been very deliberately not caring for herself. She had been working very hard not to allow herself to heal. She could see that so clearly now. All of that was beginning to affect her physically and emotionally. Her body was screaming out. Half the time, she felt as if her body was going to break into a million pieces, that it was just going to fly apart. She was filled to the limit with emotion. She couldn't handle it any more. And yet she felt paralyzed to do anything about it. Marji sensed that she was heading for a breakdown.

Marji's stalled grief touched on physical, emotional, and behavioral changes. She sensed the unresolved grief and began to question herself as to whether she had ever grieved. She did take steps toward pulling herself out of the mire. Realizing that she was heading into an emotional breakdown, Marji chose to work on her feelings about David's death. Once she reached out and began talking and exploring her feelings of guilt, she touched the anger she felt toward him for having shut her out, for not giving her a chance to help. As the guilt was redirected into anger, her movement through the storm again resumed and she worked toward resolution and healing. The physical, emotional, and behavioral changes all began to drop away as she reached out and took care of herself and her feelings of grief.

## DARLENE'S STORM

The face in the shadowed mirror seemed oddly distorted. The sunken eyes were hers, but they were glazed and sullen. There was no life in them. The mouth twisted into a sardonic smile. The lips, drawn tightly together, looked as though they might have belonged to her once. Studying the face of the stranger in the bathroom mirror, Darlene wondered how she had become so distant from herself. She couldn't remember all that had happened that had brought her to this place of nonrecognition and self-hate. Dropping to the stool, she held her head in her hands as she tried hopelessly to fit together the pieces of the puzzle that had been her life.

It started for Darlene, a 34-year-old stenographer, when her mother died of cancer. Just prior to her mother's death, she had been in Hawaii with her husband, who was on an R&R from Vietnam. Soon after she returned home, her mother had died. To understand how Darlene had come to a place of not knowing or liking herself, let's accompany her to the beginning, to the time immediately following her mother's death and the initial phases of her grieving. The time immediately after her mother's death had an unreal, numb quality and gave way to some of the physical disturbances that mark the shock stage of grief.

She remembered staring down at the freshly cooked eggs with golden slices of toast that her aunt had prepared for her; she was unable to eat. Inside she felt a heaviness that weighed on her. Her appetite, her desire to eat, was gone. Her mother was gone. The pain and suffering were finally over for her. And yet Darlene could not believe it. She had known for a long time that her mother was going to die and now that it had happened, she felt no impact. She felt nothing. None of this seemed real. She couldn't grasp it or comprehend it. She felt so alone. This sense of the unreal somehow made her nervous. Putting down the fork, she ran from the table. She could not stomach any of it.

Following her movement through the storm, we can see Darlene's experience with some of the symptoms of the searching/pining stage: uncontrollable tears, deep yearning for her mother, calling out for her, preoccupation with events surrounding the loss, and difficulty in concentration. Darlene's searching began, and the reality of her loss slowly sunk in.

The deep purple glass jar labeled "grape jelly" slid off the shelf, breaking into large, sharp pieces. Darlene had been reaching for the salt when she knocked it over. Bursting into tears, she fell into a heap in the middle of the kitchen floor. The more she looked at the purple glob staining the floor, the harder she cried. It seemed as if she broke down over nothing a lot lately. The other day she had been vacuuming and had suddenly found herself screaming out for her mother, calling to her, longing for her, missing her. Her mind constantly replayed the scene of the three of them—herself and her two sisters—arm in arm, holding each other up as they tried to help one another through the ordeal of the funeral. At work she would automatically reach for the phone, wanting to see how her mother was doing, and then remembering that she was dead. Darlene could not concentrate. On her job, her thoughts always came back to her mother. Most of the time she felt as if she were just going through the motions. She wasn't really there at all. In her place was this hollow shell of a person just marking time.

In an attempt to find her mother, to recover her loss, Darlene visited the crypt. Her search continued.

Running her hands across the hard, rough stones, she felt the crypt. If only she could touch her mother who was here, somewhere inside these thick walls. Finding cracks in between the stones, Darlene stood on her toes and peered in, hoping to catch a glimpse of her mother's dress. A moan moved from her chest as she struggled in vain to recall the dress that her mother had worn. But she couldn't even remember the color. Her mother's face, her features, the way she wore her hair—all were fading from her memory. Darlene talked to the cold crypt, hoping that somehow her mother would answer and let her know that she was near. On the edge of hysteria, Darlene searched. Her mother was missing.

Little by little she began to find her mother. Sensing her presence was one of the ways.

She pulled the long, heavy drapes open, allowing the warm sunshine to pour in through the window. Her mother had always had it this way when Darlene was a little girl. She'd liked the sunshine and flowers, pretty things. Darlene could feel her mother, standing in the bright light, her arms crossed over her chest. The presence was so strong here in the house that she loved. It was strongest in the bedroom and kitchen. Darlene liked this feeling. It was so soothing. And she felt better knowing that her mother was here where she belonged. That was nice.

Seeing her mother in a dream was another part of Darlene's finding process. In her dream, the mist floated in, and as Darlene opened her eyes, there, seated on the edge of the bed, was her mother. Glowing with radiant health, she seemed absolutely beautiful. And her lips were moving as she spoke in a soft voice that Darlene could barely hear: "See, honey—I really am okay. So you don't have to worry any more." Reaching over and stroking Darlene's hair, she praised her for the way she was taking care of things, looking after her father and little sister. As Darlene sat up in bed, her mother's image disappeared. Feeling warm and content, she rubbed her eyes. As she woke fully, she remembered that her mother had come to her, that it had been a dream—or was it?

After her mother had died, Darlene's sole intent had been to keep the family together. Setting herself aside, she began to shut off the flow of grief. Her father was falling apart, leaning on her for support. Her little sister was left neglected much of the time, so Darlene looked after her when she could. She took on the responsibility of trying to put everybody back together again. As she moved into the depression stage, she could not handle the feelings and issues there, as well as dealing with her family. There was nothing left, no energy for herself. So, as the permanence of the loss set in Darlene turned off all of her feelings.

The quiet of the hot Sunday afternoon was deafening. It was such a stifling day that the whole world seemed to be at rest. Darlene paced nervously in front of the crypt. Every Sunday she came here to visit her mother. She smiled at the irony of it. Her mother was dead. She was never coming back. She was gone forever. Yet week after week, Darlene made the pilgrimage to the crypt. For what? It was as if Darlene had taken on the duty of visiting her mother so she wouldn't feel neglected and alone. Darlene chuckled. Who deserted whom? It didn't matter. She'd made up her mind. This was it. She wasn't coming back here any more. There was no point in putting herself through this week after week. Gazing at the crypt one last time, she felt the wall of indifference rising up within her. And she said aloud, "I'm not going to think about you anymore. This is it. I'm not going to do it." At that moment she began to close off all thoughts and feelings about her mother. She turned and walked away, unfinished. And she noticed the deafening stillness of the Sunday afternoon.

Darlene carried with her a lot of anger—anger at her mother for dying and anger at her father for disrupting her private life. The anger was held inside and that locked her into this stage.

The divorce was final. Her marriage had legally ended. The sad thing was that it never really had the chance to begin. It wasn't his fault, really. He'd been home from Vietnam only a short time, but Darlene had not been there to build a life with him. "My father saw to that," she thought bitterly. He'd either show up at their apartment drunk or call her on the phone begging her to meet him. Sometimes he'd forget to go home and Darlene would rush over and pick up her little sister who had been left at home alone. Her husband had been patient at first, but when it happened time after time, he blew up at her. And it had ended. There hadn't been a chance for her private life. She rationalized away the anger she felt toward her father because of his grief. Occasionally she'd flash on angry thoughts toward her mother, who had refused to share her agony with Darlene, who had never let her get near, who had chosen to die rather than to help herself. But Darlene didn't want to think about that. She didn't want to feel that. So she locked it tightly away.

Her unresolved grief first took a physical form. She developed a thyroid problem which began to manifest itself six months after her mother's death. Prior to that she had been perfectly healthy. After a time, Darlene's father remarried. Relieved of the responsibility of taking care of him, she began to "act out" some of the anger toward her mother. She deliberately began to act in ways that her mother would have disapproved of. She stopped caring about herself, putting herself in situations that were dangerous to her personal safety. Her mire began to take the shape of self-destruction.

Within minutes her eyes adjusted to the haze and dim lights in the tavern. Sitting at the bar, she pulled her dress up, exposing her knees and a large portion of her thighs. Head tossed back, she lit up a cigarette and ordered a gin and tonic in a low, seductive voice. Having learned the pickup game well, she played it nearly every night. She had become two people, really. During working hours, dressed prim and proper, she wore the face of the normal, well-adjusted career woman. But as soon as 5 o'clock rolled around, she became faceless. Every single night she went through the same ritual. She'd go to the bar alone, meet a man, strike up a conversation, and leave with him, not even knowing his last name. Sometimes she went home with him and other times they went to her place. It was all so matter of fact. It was so cold and so impersonal. And she chuckled to herself as she thought, "Look mom, I'm doing it. Look what I'm doing!"

The self-destruction also took the form of a passive type of suicide. Darlene no longer wanted to live but felt that she could not take her own life because she was unwilling to put her sisters through that. So she set the stage for a passive death.

The stuffy bedroom resonated with echoes of death. It carried eerie sensations. Darlene pictured the broken sliding glass door at the patio. All anyone had to do was to go through the gate, come in through the patio, and right into the house. It didn't matter. Nothing mattered any more. She just did not want to go on. Darlene smiled, remembering the manager's bulging eyes as he described the murder. The last tenant, a young, single woman, had been brutally murdered in that very bedroom. And that was all right with Darlene. She had rented the place. She just didn't care. She wanted to die anyway. Suicide had been a frequent thought. But she couldn't put her sisters through that. However, they couldn't hate her for being raped and murdered. And so she lay there inviting it, waiting for it to happen.

Eventually, these self-destructive behaviors began to plague her with guilt. She felt the need to be punished. Isolating herself, she slipped more deeply into depression.

The jagged edges of the puzzle pieces were fitting together, rounding out and forming a clear picture of Darlene's life over the past two years. Piece by piece, she was beginning to see the person in the mirror. And that was what frightened her the most. Setting herself up to be murdered was scary enough, but what about the physical abuse and the bar scenes and the long succession of men? That person looking back at her was a tramp, in her eyes. A sense of deep shame welled up inside her. Everyone knew about her, what she had become. No longer could she hold her head up and look people in the eye. Rising from the stool, she confronted the image in the mirror. "You're so bad. You are such a filthy person. You don't deserve to even be around people. You should be locked away."

Her seclusion began with a move to an upstairs apartment in a neighborhood where no one knew her. She lived upstairs so that no one could see in. She kept the drapes tightly drawn so that she couldn't see out. Becoming like her mother before her illness, Darlene made herself a prisoner in her own home. All she wanted to do was sleep. But she had to work to support herself. That became a monumental effort. Constantly she called in sick at work. People from work came to the door to check on her because she never answered the phone. She didn't want to deal with people. So in the morning when she did go to work, she'd rush down the stairs and jump into her car before anyone had the chance to speak or catch her eye. And she'd perform the same rite in the evening. To do her laundry, she'd force herself to get up very early in the morning, while the rest of the people in the apartment complex slept. Once the man next door, who seemed nice, had asked her over for a drink. In her isolation, she'd lost her social skills. She didn't know what to say. She stammered enough to put him off for the moment. And the next week she had moved.

Stranded in the depression stage, Darlene's grief took physical, emotional, and very dangerous self-destructive avenues. During the bar-scene period, she acted out some of the anger. Then she was left with guilt. With the need to punish herself, she withdrew into seclusion. After two years in hiding she came to realize that she was becoming her mother, taking on her behaviors just prior to her illness and death. Like her mother, she was in hiding with the drapes pulled, withholding feelings, and isolating herself from the world.

Then Darlene decided that she *wasn't* her mother. She was Darlene. And she knew that she didn't want to die. Slowly, carefully, she began reaching out, forming meaningful relationships and rebuilding her life. It was as though having become her mother for two years, having punished herself for her anger, she was finally able to let go of the anger and guilt toward her mother. Once she let the feelings go, she was able to release her mother and start putting her life back together.

Journeying with Marji and Darlene through the process and into the mire of their grief, we have witnessed the incredibly self-destructive forms that unresolved grief can take in our lives. Being lodged in the mire can turn into a life-threatening condition. It can become dangerous and jeopardize our health and well-being. What causes us to get stuck?

## WHAT HOLDS US IN THE MIRE?

The intertwining of cultural taboos and intrapersonal dynamics can hold us in the mire.

## Cultural Taboos

Earlier we saw how cultural attitudes and messages could work toward halting our passage through the storm of grief. We live in a culture that does not encourage or support the expression of grief. Underlying this is a taboo that forbids the open expression of feelings. These taboos, lurking underground, become insidious. They've been around hiding among the shadows for hundreds of years. Our parents' parents and their parents' parents learned these taboos long ago; they've been handed down from generation to generation. We learn about life and how to deal with the different aspects of it from our parents, who teach us the way their parents taught them. So as little children we learn, and as parents we teach.

As we learn the attitudes, messages, and taboos that are the heritage of our culture, we take them in, we internalize them, and they become our own. In this way they become our intrapersonal dynamics, our own personality traits. Some of these dynamics can surface and interfere with our natural ability to grieve. They can interrupt the flow of our storm and hold us in the mire.

## Intrapersonal Dynamics

Intrapersonal dynamics refer to specific personality traits that may predispose us toward staying lodged in one of the stages of grief. These traits that we've absorbed from our culture are learned ways of coping and dealing with the world. Those that might disrupt the flow of grief include not showing feelings; not *feeling* feelings; not expressing feelings, especially those of anger and guilt; not being able to build meaningful relationships; and not being able to reach out.

### Not Showing Feelings

As children we learn how to be in the world in a variety of ways. Through the example of our parents, in our interaction with our peers, from the mouths of our teachers and older siblings, on the movie and television screens, we are given indirect messages about how to cope with feelings.

In childhood, if we are told that anger or tears are somehow "wrong" or "bad" we quickly learn to hide them away. Many of us are given the message "Be strong." When a little boy falls down and hurts himself or cries out in anger and frustration, he is told, "Big boys don't cry." And so begins his basic training on being strong. Strength is seen as not showing feelings. Tears are tolerated with little girls; there is the implicit message that crying is all right for little girls because they are so small and weak. And so little girls learn to be "weak" and show some feelings. However, outbursts of anger from little girls are stifled and considered "unladylike." And anger becomes a feeling that little girls are not supposed to show.

Through these types of messages, woven into the different facets of our culture, we learn not to show feelings. In hiding our feelings we reject them. They become foreign to us. They become our enemies. In hiding them, we grow afraid. If we're afraid of feelings, moving through grief where we have to confront them will be very difficult. Our tendency will be to do what we've always done—hide them away from ourselves. And in doing so, we shut off the flow of our grief and are caught in the mire.

### Not Feeling Feelings

When we hide our feelings away, we don't experience them. This is reinforced in our culture. An example of one of the ways that this reinforcement occurs can be seen in parents' reactions when a child loses a loved pet. In order to protect the child from the hurt of loss, the parents may immediately replace the lost animal with another. The message beneath this action is, "Don't feel sad, don't cry, don't feel your loss. Your loss can be replaced." The need to *feel* our feelings is passed over. The well-meaning parents with intentions of shielding the child from hurt actually rob the child of a basic part of being human, the ability to feel. Because we are deprived of our human need to grieve, we do not learn how to mourn. If we don't know how to mourn as children, we will not know how to mourn as adults.

> We know that the ability to handle life's vicissitudes is tied to childhood experiences. Research shows that individuals who experience loss in the years before adolescence are especially pregnable to loss later. The child does not know how to mourn or is taught to "be a good boy or girl" and not to mourn. Grief gets frozen within . . .[39]

### Not Expressing Feelings

Another personality trait that might inhibit the flow of grief is the inability to own and express feelings—particularly anger and guilt. Anger and guilt are billed as negative emotions in our culture and their expression is forbidden. As we grow up, we may be slapped, screamed at, or sent to our rooms without supper for an outburst of anger. Its expression, in any form, is not permitted. And so we learn to disown our anger. "Nice people do not get angry." Anger and violence have become synonymous in our culture. Disowning anger, we've grown afraid of it and it has become distorted. We learn that anger is destructive. We are afraid that if we allow ourselves our anger, we will hurt and destroy. The irony is that within the soil of *disowned* anger lie the seeds of violence. Violence grows out of stored-up anger. If we own our anger and learn to express it in direct, appropriate ways as we feel it, instead of storing it up, the weeds of violence will die out.

We learn early that the expression of anger is inappropriate. We learn early to close it off from consciousness. Guilt is the other direction of anger. So if we disavow anger, we cut off guilt. Since anger and guilt are prominent emotions in the depression stage and since releasing them is a necessity in order to move on, a learned ability to supress these feelings will deter our ability to flow through this stage. And we can become stuck.

### Inability to Build Meaningful Relationships

Being unable to build intimate relationships with others is another trait that can hinder our natural process of grief. Severe emotional trauma in early childhood usually sets in motion the variables for the development of this trait. It happens when a young child attempts to touch and build satisfying relationships, but experiences rejection and a sense of loss in return. Through this, the child learns to fear closeness to other people; closeness is unpleasant, and it hurts. So this child becomes an adult who is suspicious and wary of other people. The lack of trust keeps other people at a distance. It doesn't allow them to get close, where they can hurt. Life becomes empty and the person is walled off from self and from other people. Here, a lifestyle of depression may be adopted. There is no flow of feelings in this style of living. To feel means to hurt, so emotions are cut off. Add to this empty life the thunder of loss and the storm of grief, and it is likely that the void will widen. With no support system, with no one to turn to for comfort, the person is left alone in incredible despair. The flow of feelings was stopped before the loss ever occurred. So it is highly unlikely that the feelings of grief will be allowed to move. With no one to lend a shoulder to cry on, with no permission to feel grief, coupled with the hopelessness already inherent in this lifestyle, the suicidal ideation that is a part of normal grief may take on grotesque proportions. Staying stuck, alone in this desperation, the person may begin to look at suicide as a way out of the pain of living.

### Inability to Reach Out

Related to the personality characteristic of being unable to form satisfying relationships is the inability to reach out, to ask for help and comfort, to allow other people to know that their support and caring is needed. This trait seems to be common in those of us who are caretakers. Caretakers spend much of their time and energy taking care of the needs of other people. Caretakers have grown up in the tradition that said that being strong and stable is the same as being a good person. Indirectly there is the message that showing feelings is essentially weak and is not okay. Growing up projecting this image of stability and strength, the caretaker quickly becomes the one who others turn to with their feelings and problems. With this reinforcement, caretakers come to believe that they are strong and stable; their feelings of self-worth grow out of living within this role. In seeing themselves as the nurturing force for other people, caretakers' needs for sharing feelings and showing vulnerability are constantly put aside. Needing others is perceived as being synonymous with being weak or bad.

Women tend to become caretakers. This may come from the message we received as children that said that girls are weak because they show emotions of hurt. Becoming a caretaker may be our way of showing the world that we are not weak, but strong. The end result of caretaking is that a whole part of our personality may be cut off from consciousness—the part that hurts sometimes, too, the part that needs comfort and care from time to time. When we are caretakers and need support, we find it difficult to reach out and ask for help. To show our vulnerability is to admit that we are not *always* strong and stable, that we are not *always* okay. This puts us in direct conflict with our carefully built self-image that feeds our feelings of worthiness. So reaching out becomes an almost impossible task.

In terms of grieving, this presents a problem. Even if there is a support system, which caretakers usually have, it is not used because of the inability to reach out. So caretakers attempt to become stronger, trying to maintain control, trying to carry the weight of grief alone. To maintain control, the feelings are banished. This cutting off of the feelings once again will interrupt the flow of the process of grief and will trap us in the mire.

These personality traits may be some of the intrapersonal dynamics involved that interfere with the natural flow of grief. There probably are many more. For this reason, further research and study is needed in this area of grieving.

The perfume from the tiny pink blossoms drifted through the trees, adding a sweet scent to the air. The day was warm and gentle. The wind brushed wistfully against her cheek. It was Mother's Day. It had been five years since Darlene had stood at the crypt. She'd been drawn out here today, her heart full of things that needed expression. "Mom," she began shyly, "I'm alive. I feel. And you know what? Feeling is not so bad. I think I'm growing, really growing. Now I can cry, scream, and yell. And it's okay. No more holding it all inside. It feels so good. I know what it's like to *feel* now. I'm reaching out more now. My friends really care. I'm alive, Mom. I can't allow myself to die the way you did. I'm not you. I'm me. And I feel so very sad inside that you didn't know there was another way. But there is. It's choosing to live, Mom. It's the way of searching for myself, trying to find out who I am. It's the way of caring about myself. It's the way of *feeling* the feelings whether they hurt or feel good. I'm learning to care for *me*. I'm learning to love *me*. I wish you could be here to share this. Sometimes I still miss you so much. And, Mom, I love you." Placing the bouquet at the crypt, Darlene turned and saw the figure of the man she loved in the distance. And as she walked away, finished at last, she released herself from the past. A bright smile lit up her face, and she ran up the hill, away from the past.

Darlene had been perilously trapped within the mire. With the flow of her feelings interrupted, her life was in danger in various ways. Once the movement of her feelings began again, she pulled herself out of the mire and completed her journey through grief. Flowing with our feelings of grief takes us around the deep pools of mire toward a place of healing. We've seen how the disruption of that flow can lead us into the mire. Being stuck there can be very hazardous. We've looked at the dangerous directions that unresolved grief can follow, as well as some of the factors that hold us in the mire. In this section we'll search for ways to tell if we're stuck. We'll investigate means for avoiding the mire and find paths for creating flow and movement again.

## HOW CAN WE TELL IF WE'RE STUCK IN THE MIRE?

How do we know if we're lodged within our process of grief, stalled, not moving? While there's a general picture of the grief process, each of us will travel on our own individual journey through the storm. Even the timetable for passing through grief is different for each of us. We all have our own inner clocks that we follow. So there is no distinct formula that shows that we are lodged within our process. However, there are things that we can do that may point out our entrapment in the mire. We can listen to ourselves, and we can look in the direction of our actions.

## Listening to Ourselves

Tuning in to our intuition, being in touch with and listening to what is going on inside, can tell us if we are caught in the mire. There are some specific things to listen for. If it's been a long time since our loss—say, one year, maybe two—and the pain has in no way lightened, then this may be a sign that our movement through the process has stopped. If we feel the same devastation and intensity that we experienced right after the loss with no changes, with no lessening of the pain, we may be stuck.

If we hear messages or receive images or flashes from inside that make us feel trapped or blocked, or a sense of "spinning our wheels," our intuition may be telling us that we are stuck.

Tuning in to our feelings and hearing what they are saying to us is the way we listen to ourselves. It is important to stop and quiet ourselves, getting into a relaxed state so that our feelings can be heard, so that they can "talk" to us. We need to ask them to speak to us from this place of calm and stillness. What do they say? Stay still. Ask. And then wait for the answer to come. It will, if we are quiet and patient. Ask: What am I feeling now about my loss? How does the whole of it feel? What is the total feeling tone of it all? Sit quietly and allow it to come. You will know when the answer you're seeking is there. You will recognize it. If you get answers that don't seem to fit, just remain quiet and stay with it until the answer comes. You'll know when it's right because you'll feel it. It will feel right deep inside. If you are caught in the mire, you will feel and hear that loud and clear. It is through tuning in, asking, and trusting yourself to answer that you can listen to what is going on inside.

Since our feelings live in the body, listening to the messages our bodies send us in the physical route is another pathway for finding if we're stuck. If a long time has lapsed since our loss and in the meantime we've developed things like ulcers, migraine headaches, asthma, or intestinal distress, our bodies may be trying to send us the message that something is wrong, that the flow of our feelings is blocked and is showing itself physically. If we've been to the doctor with frequent ailments since our loss, this may be an indication that our grief has taken a wrong turn. An increase in illness or symptoms of disease may also be warning signs. Become quiet and still. Relax your body a little bit at a time. Get in touch with your body. Now ask yourself: Where do I feel this grief in my body? Listening in on yourself will tell you where you are. It will tell you if you are stuck.

## Looking in the
## Direction of Our Actions

Not only do we need to get in touch with ourselves, our bodies, and our emotions, we also need to look in the *direction* of our actions. Changes in behavior are a part of the natural process of grief. But prolonged, exaggerated, dangerous, self-destructive behaviors that seem to increase after the passage of a year or two indicate the snare of the mire. We are considering behaviors that are occurring a year or longer after the loss.

Has there been an increase in self-destructive behaviors that may be ways of anesthetizing your pain? Is there a noticeable increase in the amount you're drinking, drugs you're taking, food you're eating, that began after your loss occurred? Are you needing pills to make you sleep at night? Are you taking pills to get yourself going in the morning? What directions has your behavior taken? Are your actions drastically different and more destructive than they were before your loss?

Are you experiencing overwhelming thoughts and fantasies about killing yourself? Are these thoughts and impulses that are constantly plaguing you rather than being occasional fleeting thoughts and impulses? Have you made any suicide attempts? This direction indicates deeply troubled waters. It is a warning that you are in need of bereavement intervention. If the movement of your life has stopped to the point where you no longer want to live, then seek out help. You need someone to help you, to intervene with your grief, to help you get the process flowing. It means searching out professional help, individual counseling, or psychotherapy so you can begin to work through the stalled feelings of grief. Your door out of the box of suicide may be hooking up with individual therapists or bereavement groups, people who understand grieving who can allow you the space to feel it.

Has your behavior become increasingly bizarre or strange in the time span since your loss? Are you doing destructive kinds of things that you've never done before? Do you seem to be living with a stranger inside you who is behaving in unusual ways? Do you feel that you are now a stranger to the person you were before the loss?

Have you cried over your loss? Or have you maintained a face of stoicism and composure? Have you felt or expressed anger about your loss? Or have you been holding tight the reigns of control, riding herd over your feelings, keeping them in line, keeping them in storage? Are you walking through life feeling absolutely nothing? Do you find that you've had no heart reaction to your loss, that you haven't felt any feelings of grief?

Are you "speeding" as a way of keeping feelings at bay? Speeding is a way of behaving in which we don't feel, mainly because we don't give ourselves time to feel. Speeding was seen by Freidman and Rosenmann, two researchers of cardiovascular disease. In their study of personality profiles of patients with heart disease, they dubbed the individual who suffers from "hurry sickness" as "Type A."[40] This involves a lifestyle in which we continually need to be moving, rushing, doing, accomplishing. We are forever caught up in any activity as long as it is constructive. Here is a description of this behavior:

> [Such a person] may create undue time pressure for himself in tasks ranging from getting out the report, cleaning out the attic, beating the commuter traffic home at night, to swimming his daily exercise laps in the pool. His competition with the clock is unrelieved and although the Type A person may win minor skirmishes, time pressures inevitably leave the Type A man (or woman) frustrated, nervous, hostile, and even more determined to accomplish more in less time.[41]

The dynamic at work here is to rush, to do, to hurry, with an increasing inability to slow down and relax. The image comes to mind of a hamster in the cage running on the wheel, going nowhere, just constantly running. The running, the turning of the wheel in perpetual circles, faster and faster, may be a defense against feeling. It may be a way to close off feelings. If the constant motion slows down or stops, if our time isn't crammed full of activity, if we slow down and relax, feelings may begin to stir inside. They may begin to bubble up, sneak up on us, and catch us off guard. The point of speeding is to outrun the feelings so that we don't have to feel them. If this description fits, it may be a signal that our feelings of grief are blocked up somewhere, not moving. It may be a sign that we are trying to keep them at a distance. Our mourning may have stopped and we may be stranded.

After a long period of time there are other questions to ask that may point to unresolved grief. Do you feel that the passage of time has not healed the wounds of loss? Does your life seem to be steadily falling apart as time passes, rather than being put back together? After all this time are you still feeling half instead of whole? Are you empty and dead inside, no longer gaining any pleasure from life? The answers to these questions will give you a sense of where you are with your grief.

## HOW CAN WE AVOID GETTING CAUGHT IN THE MIRE?

Armed with some of the warning signs, we can discover if we're stuck. Bein entrenched within the mire is a life-threatening condition. But when we lose w must grieve. So how can we avoid getting stuck in the mire? In order to bypass the mire, we must stay with the flow of our process and we must encounter it.

## Staying with the Flow

Staying with the flow means staying with our grief. Since the storm brings with it raging winds, pouring rains, and great turbulance, the temptation to run for cover, to hide away from it, is very strong. We must not give in to this temptation and push our grief away. To sidestep the mire, we must stay in and with our flow of grief. It is crucial to stave off the impulse to delay feeling the pain or to shut it off. There are some things we can do during the initial weeks of our storm to keep the flow moving.

Staying with our grief means staying away from things that will shut down our feelings. Do not allow yourself to be drugged or sedated because you are upset over your loss. Of course you are upset—you've suffered a loss. And you need to feel it. Often, doctors who are trying to spare us from the deep hurt and turbulance of mourning will prescribe tranquilizers or sleeping pills to get us comfortably through the initial weeks of grieving. These drugs mask our pain and help us to push it away. Dulling ourselves to the feelings of loss through the use of alcohol or any other drug will allow us to shut off the grief. It will be a detriment later on. It is in the feelings of loss that our movement through grief happens. If we delay or stop the flow of feelings, then our pain cannot lessen. Being drugged is a pitfall because it is an easy way to shut down grief; this will take us down into the mire. Once we stop the flow of grief, it is difficult to get it moving again. Stay with grief. Embrace the pain of loss, because it is through the pain that we heal.

Stay with grief by remaining in your familiar environment, even if staying there reminds you of the loss. Many people leave their homes or move shortly after traumatic loss. It is usually a way to escape the memories. Be courageous enough to stay there at least for a year. Be reminded so that the loss can become real. It is through experiencing the reality of loss that we move into dealing with it, taking a step toward its resolution. Staying in your familiar environment will keep you with the flow.

Stay with grief by holding on to the mementos that remind you of your loss. Don't whisk them away out of sight to make you forget. Remember, you've lost something or someone precious. Remember the part that your loss played in your life and grieve because it is no longer there. Remember, so that you can be in the pain. Remember, so that you can journey through it and eventually emerge on the other side of it. Keep the mementos for as long as you need them. Your intuition will guide you; trust it. Don't allow those around you who are trying to spare you your pain to hide the mementos away. Gently but firmly let them know that you need these things around for a while because you need the pain to help you heal. Staying with the flow, the motion of our dance with grief, will keep us out of the mire and moving in the direction of healing and wholeness.

## Encountering Grief

Encountering our grief means to meet with it, to let it into our lives, and to go with it. Grief comes in waves, rushing over us, engulfing us. One way of encountering our grief is to go along with the waves. Many times as we are doing routine tasks such as washing the dishes or grocery shopping, a wave of tears will suddenly surge up and wash over us. Ride these waves. Go with them as they come, with the understanding that the waves are simply part of the normal flow of grief. There's no need to run from them in fear. Just let them be. Rather than trying to maintain control by stopping them, let tears fall freely. There is no need to be in control or maintain composure at this time, because we are hurting—hurting from the wound of loss.

Encountering our process means allowing the tears their beauty. There is no need to be ashamed of our tears. They purify us and cleanse us as the pain flows out and away. Showing our tears is showing the tender, beautiful side that makes human beings magnificent creatures. There is no need to wear the false, strong stoic mask. Meeting the storm is being within it, in its rain and wind, in the vulnerability of our tears. The people who love us will understand and accept. Those who can't are not our concern. Our concern is nurturing and allowing the part of us that is tender and hurt to *be*. It is letting ourselves be where we are. And in being ourselves, we allow the flowing of our feelings inside to show through to the outside world. We allow that to be okay because *we* are okay. There is no need to hide. Being in our process keeps us clear of the mire.

Encountering the storm means touching and being touched. It is all about letting our grief touch us through its expression. We need to express the hurt, the anger, the guilt. We need to verbalize it, to say it aloud, to say out loud all the feelings, thoughts, memories that are bouncing around inside us, seeking expression. Once they flow from our lips, they are released. No longer are they carried around festering inside. And as we express them, little by little, the burden will gently lift. In allowing our feelings to touch us, we'll grow lighter instead of being pulled into the depths by the weight of locked-up feelings. Touching, letting people know that we are hurting, invites others to give us the gifts of connection and comfort. In touching we share with those who can listen. We cry with those who can hold us and cry with us. We share our anger with those who can accept. In touching we ask for what we need. We reach out, ask, and take it in. In touching we ask others to help us to keep with our grief away from the mire. Encountering our grief will keep us from stumbling into the traps that lie within the mire.

The storm can create the dark pools of mud that can hold us captive. But if we keep with the flow of our grief and continue to encounter it along the way, we can avoid getting stuck in the mire.

It may happen that we do not avoid the mire and after a time we find ourselves stranded, stuck within our grief. What can we do to free ourselves?

## HOW TO CREATE FLOW
## AND GET MOVING AGAIN

Flowing with and through the feelings of grief is the third ingredient in the formula. In order to live with loss, we must be able to flow with it. Flow is the ingredient for getting past the mire. Flow is the motion through our journey of unfolding. If we become stuck or stranded within our grief, the way to free ourselves and get moving again is to *create flow*.

Flow is movement. It is the motion of the dance. To dance with and through our feelings of grief, we need freedom, the free space in which to glide and bend and twirl and turn. Flow is the freedom of movement.

To create flow we need to create a climate in which motion is free and unencumbered, a climate where nothing interrupts, obstructs, or stops motion. To create a climate for flow we must remove any blocks, walls, or barricades that prevent uninhibited motion. Exercises that can help us create flow and begin movement through our unfolding process are exploring the blocks to grieving, brick-wall imagery, and having a dialogue with the body.

Exploring Blocks to Grieving.    In order to create flow, we need to remove any blocks that may be interrupting our movement. So picture in your mind's eye the blocks that stand before you, disrupting your movement through grief. Take a few minutes now to be with them, learning all you can about them. (Give yourself a few minutes.) Now describe how they look. How many are there? Give them size, shape, color, texture. Name the blocks and list them below.

Begin a dialogue with these blocks, taking them aside one at a time. Ask why they are here, what their function is. Record their replies.

Teach them each how you *feel* about them being in your way—blocking you from moving through the healing work of grief.

Record their reply.

Tell them that you no longer need them. Picture how you are going to remove these blocks. Describe the ways in which you are going to overcome and move each one.

Brick-Wall Imagery. This is an exercise for removing walls that are obstructing our flow. To do this exercise either talk the instructions into a tape recorder and take yourself through the imagery as you play it back or read through it, recording your experience as you go along.

Make yourself very comfortable now, uncrossing your arms and legs. Closing your eyes, take in a deep breath, in through the nose and out through the mouth, and another in through the nose and out through the mouth, and still another in through the nose and out through the mouth. Feel your body relaxing and relaxing, feel all tension and tightness, all the garbage you don't need, falling out and away as you continue to breathe, in through the nose and out through the mouth. Feel more and more relaxed with every breath you take, relaxing and relaxing and relaxing. Now feel yourself going deeper as you see a winding staircase in front of you. Begin to descend the stairs, going deeper, relaxing and relaxing. At the bottom of the stairway you can see a brick wall—a wall that is keeping you separated from yourself, a wall that keeps you stagnant and stuck. Now, slowly approach that wall and begin to study it. How big is it? What does it look like? What color is it? What is it made out of? Reach out and touch it. Is it rough? Smooth? What is its texture?

Feeling around the brick wall, running your hands over its surface, find a loose brick—one that is not cemented in very lightly, one whose mortar has broken free; work the brick out of the wall. Feel it as it slides along quite easily in your hand as you pull it from the wall. Now get into that brick. Become it. Take on its color, size, shape, and texture. Know what it feels like to be this brick. Stay aware of how you are feeling. Answer the questions that I am going to ask in the first person, because you are the brick. What are you? (Give yourself some blank tape time to allow the answer to come.) Why are you a part of this wall that is blocking my movement through grief? Why are you stopping me? (Give yourself more blank tape time to allow a response to come.)

What do you know as the brick that you did not know as yourself? What are you learning about this wall that is holding you back? (Give yourself some time.)

Ask the brick how you can join together. Ask what you can do so the two of you can work together and move on. Make a pact with the brick. Join forces. (Give youself some blank tape time.)

Now, find the next loose brick. Carefully work it free of the wall and become it, taking on its characteristics, its color, size, shape, and texture. As you become the brick, ask: What are you? Why are you stopping the flow? What else are you learning about this wall that is holding you back? (Give yourself some time.)

Ask the brick what you can do so that the two of you can join together and move on. Again, make a pact with the brick. Join forces. (Give yourself some time.) Continue with this, brick by brick, until the wall no longer can support itself, until it topples and falls down.

As you see the wall crumbling, feel the freedom as the flow once again begins its movement. Know that you have become one and have made peace with the things that made up the wall, with those elements that obstructed your flow. Now join hands with all of your bricks and jump into the flowing motion of grief; allow it to carry you toward a healing place. Feel the lightness and the freedom of the motion. Soak it in. (Give yourself some blank tape time to be with this.)

Now, slowly begin to climb back up the spiral staircase, ascending upward, higher and higher. When you reach the top and feel ready, open your eyes and come back into this room feeling wonderfully refreshed and relaxed.

Record your experiences with this exercise. How did you feel? What did you learn? How does the flow feel?

**Having a Dialogue with the Body.**   Sometimes the body throws up barricades that stop our motion. We can locate the blockage in areas of the body in which we are feeling tension or tightness. Since the body is the house in which our feelings live, stuck windows or squeaky doors or loose floorboards can show us where a block is. These places that need attention and repair show up in the form of aches and pains, tension knots and sore spots. My first experience with a dialogue with my body happened one evening after I'd gone on a class field trip to the local crisis clinic. When I got home my eyes ached terribly. I closed them and they throbbed with tension. I had heard about having a dialogue with the body in an encounter group, so I decided to try it.

The way to have a dialogue with your body is to focus on an area within your body that is tense or aching. Get yourself into a relaxed state, bringing all of your consciousness to the place of distress. Feel the pain there. Feel the aching. Experience the tightness, experience the way your body feels there. Become the pain and discomfort. Feel it and get into it. Now ask that part of your body—your aching back or your hurting head—What are you trying to tell me? What message do you want to get across? I'm listening now. Stay very quiet, waiting for the answer. Other thoughts may come up and through in the meantime. Don't try to stop them, just let these upper layers of thoughts come through. Wait, patiently, until your body answers. Ask again. Remain open and receptive to what it is trying to tell you. The answer may come in the form of a picture or an image. Or it may come as a thought or message. You will recognize it when it does appear.

In my case the message that came was that my eyes did not want to see. Once you get an answer, lift it up and look underneath and see what's there. Try to get further information concerning the message you were given. You might ask, What are you about? What else is there to you? What's that underneath you? The question I asked was, What is it that you didn't want to see? The answer came swiftly. It was all about feelings of revulsion and anger from the trip to the crisis clinic that I was hiding, that I didn't want to see. The visit had been a disturbing experience. The place was very cold and antiseptic. People in distress and emotional pain were being herded through like cattle. The paperwork and their bodies were being attended to, but no one seemed to care about their feelings. I felt angry and revolted by the lack of humanity and sensitivity I saw there. Instead of owning these feelings and expressing them, I locked them away. I didn't want to look at them. As soon as I "saw" the feelings that I'd disowned, and let them be okay, the tension and tightness and pain left my eyes. As I unlocked the feelings and let them flow, I unlocked my eyes.

When you get to what is underneath it, what it's all about, then ask that area what you need to do to release the blockage. Again, wait for an answer in patience and acceptance. It will come. This is a powerful, beautiful exercise that connects us to the wells of wisdom that flow within our bodies.

Another way of creating the flow through the body is through bodywork. Bodywork is a new form of therapy that removes blocks through different forms of body manipulation and massage. There are certified practitioners trained to locate and remove areas of tension that are blocking the flow of energy through the body. Usually with the release of tension comes the release of feelings that were stored there. Some body therapies are *shiatsu*, a Japanese form of massage; *acupressure*, a form of massage that utilizes the acupuncture points of the body to redirect blocked energy flow; *trager*, a soft form of massage that relieves stress and tension; *rolphing*, a realignment of the body through the manipulation of facia, the tissue around the muscles; and *lomi work*, a form that combines the techniques of deep muscle massage, rolphing, and acupressure to release stopped energy, and Gestalt therapy, to integrate the feelings that bubble up and flow out. Seeking out trained professionals in these areas are another way to create flow.

Creating flow is all about discovering and removing the blocks, walls, and barricades that obstruct the flow and movement of our energy and feelings. Flow is vital. It keeps us vibrant and alive.

In Chapter Three, we've encountered the mire, the consequences and dangers of becoming stuck there, factors that can push us in that direction, ways to tell if we're stuck, how to avoid it and how to get out of it. We've seen flow, what it is, how it feels. And, as the third ingredient in our formula for living with loss, we've come to understand how its creation can help us to pass through the mire.

In "The Clearing," Chapter Four, we will investigate the other side of grief, the healing, whole side. We will look at what grief can teach, how loss and gain are transformed into each other. It will also introduce the fourth ingredient in the formula and probe the meaning of living with loss.

# THE CLEARING

The young, vital face filling the TV screen was lit up with that familiar Irish wit and charm. Entranced by the smiling face from the dated newsreel, I zoomed back through time, through the memories, through almost two decades to Black Friday. It was hard to comprehend that so much time had passed. Coming back to the present and taking another look from this perspective, the face seemed oddly different, slightly out of place, as if it no longer belonged in this time. And it didn't. Shaken and jolted on that Friday so long ago, a common loss was shared by a nation as the result of a deadly bullet that found its mark. Now children learn about that day from history books. For me, Black Friday was devastating. It has survived clearly in my memories. The wind was knocked out of me as his burning flame was so abruptly snuffed away. The world was turned upside down. And now children regard that day as just another fact to commit to memory for the next history test. It seems to have come full-circle. Everything seems different now. Back then, the world was filled with pain and doom. My heart ached for the First Lady shrouded behind the black veil. And the image of little John-John, too young to grasp the impact of the loss, saluting his father's casket, tore me apart inside. I was frightened for them, concerned about how they'd ever live through the shock and pain. I was frightened at my own sense of emptiness and wondered if I, and the nation, would survive this tragedy.

Everything was broken dreams, hurt, fear, and confusion. And now the face on the screen no longer fits. We've all changed and grown into a new time. John and Caroline are now young adults, leading their own lives. And Jackie has built herself a new and different life. The nation has moved forward and stepped backward. The pain and the loss that we all shared seems distant, left in the past, with the face on the screen. The wheel of life continues to spin with endings and beginnings, beginnings and endings.

As the clouds of the storm pass overhead and begin to move on, the sun's healing rays dry up the pools of the mire. All things in nature begin to take on a clean, clear crispness. The sky wears colors of brilliant, cloudless blue, blending with the cool green of the trees that dot the foreground. The aromatic smells of nature fill the air with freshness after the storm. A nation was rocked and shaken by the explosive thunder that was the loss of a beloved leader. The beginnings of the raucous storm that is grief was shared. Passing through the storm, we came into the clearing, that place which lies on the other side of grief.

Once the storm of grief has passed, a sense of healing seems to have taken place. Our new perceptions of our lives seem to take on a new clarity. All our senses seem to be renewed and enriched. The clearing that follows the storm of grief leads us into a state of warmth, freshness, and sunshine. It's a state of being in which the gap in our life's circle has been filled in. Within this wholeness is the ability to reach outward and risk and give away parts of ourselves, once again, to the world.

The clearing is a luscious green meadow, resting on a plateau where we can gaze all around and see clearly. It is a place where, having passed through the storm, we can look back and see our lives stretched out before, after, and during the loss, without the feeling of searing pain. It is a place where we can see it all so clearly with a sense of quiet peace and acceptance. And from this vantage point, we begin to see the growth and gains that have sprung from our loss. The dawning of a fresh understanding of the oneness of loss and gain is experienced on a deep level. Insight into the mystery of grief, its turbulence and pain, change to growth, insight, and new awareness. The clearing is the place where our growth and gains begin to be realized and integrated into the more unified circle of our lives. It is a place where we once again feel complete, whole, and alive.

From this clearing on the other side of grief, we'll see how our process of unfolding teaches and how loss and gain are transformed into one and then the other and back again. We'll look at ways to use the process of grief for growth and insight, and will introduce the fourth ingredient in the formula: creating a climate for opening. And within this, we'll arrive at an understanding of what living with loss means.

# GRIEF AS A TEACHER

Grief is a teacher. As we flow with it, shattered and torn, and into it, tossing and turning and through it, twisting and winding, we encounter multiple lessons that need to be learned. It is as though in passing through all of this we are somehow reshaped, as grief teaches us about ourselves. It shows us ghosts we've been afraid to meet. It hands us the broom to sweep out the dusty cobwebs and sleeping bats that have been locked away in our inner attics. It throws open window shades and sashes and lets the sunshine highlight sparkling jewels that we didn't even know we had. It waits patiently with us as we unravel the tangled mystery that is ourself, uncovering dormant talents and qualities. As we move through grief and learn the lessons there, we begin to change and to find new directions and insights. Come with me now and follow me into the rooms that contain my lesson. Share what the journey through the storms of grief are teaching me.

My first journey through the storm of grief led me to search out the hidden closets where I had locked away the demons I didn't want to confront. The path took me to facing the first demon, the possibility of having a life-threatening disease, multiple sclerosis. I surrendered myself to the battle and I survived, carrying away many lessons.

The first thing that I discovered was that I am not immune to loss. Loss is a part of all nature and since I also fit into nature's scheme, loss is an aspect of the cycle of my life. I realized that permanence is an illusion. I live in time and space and since time passes, so does everything within time. All things will pass; nothing in life is permanent. Sometimes I forget to remember that. And that too is a part of my journey.

In dealing with my multiple sclerosis, I came face to face with the demon, the fear about my own death, the anger and sorrow that I am going to die. Passing through the feelings, I released the illusion of my own immortality. I absorbed the reality that death will touch me; it will claim me because although death is not at all fair, it just *is*. I became grounded in the fact that the *now*, each present moment, is all that any of us have. So the *now* is what has to be embraced and experienced fully. Sometimes still, I forget to remember that.

In the process of facing my demon and letting go of the illusion of immortality, I freed my captive feelings about my own death and the feelings about having a life-threatening disease. During this process, I left behind the symptoms of M.S. It seems as if I no longer needed them. From the clearing I have asked myself, "Why did I give myself those symptoms? What did I need to learn?" From the clearing I can see the answer. I'd spent a large portion of my life running away from the pain of loss, locking it away deep down inside. I was cutting myself off from a very important part of me, my feelings. As a result, I grew into being a "strong" person, an *unfeeling* person. I didn't show weakness by allowing myself to be vulnerable. I didn't show my anger when people used me. I kept quiet and felt powerless and terribly used. After all, I was strong. I could take it. I hid out in my head a lot. I seemed to live from the neck up—rationalizing, analyzing, but not feeling. I was strong, protected, and invulnerable. I was wandering through my life a very scared person, but not knowing that, I was bumbling along, only half human. I was not whole and complete. I spent a lot of years building the walls and it would take something catastrophic to penetrate them. I needed a way to get through the walls that protected the demon. I needed a way to face the demon in which I couldn't run and hide. So I gave myself a life-death situation, multiple sclerosis symptoms from which there was no escape. I chose to give myself those symptoms to force me to begin to confront my feelings about the losses in my life and my feelings about the greatest loss of all, my own life, my *be*-ing. Looking back, I wonder how many of those symptoms were warning signals from my body that I was dangerously stuck in the mire. The catastrophe of not having control over my body did break through the walls. In wrestling with the demon, my journey began. This was my beginning, my way of learning to live with loss. And it seems that the journey goes on and on and on. Sometimes I forget to remember.

Wrestling with the demon was only the beginning. Now I had other monsters to contend with. The first door I unlocked and opened led to other closed doors, other rooms where I had hidden feelings amongst the dust and cobwebs. I found that any time that I locked something away in dark, hidden places by denial and avoidance, it took on more power, it became bigger and more frightening. My hidden fears and feelings about my own death transformed themselves into an overpowering, fire-breathing dragon. My locked-up feelings about other losses in my life changed into other monsters. So my journey continued on and took me back to each loss that had been locked away. As I opened each door to each room, I had to free the feelings by grieving each loss. I had to finish with each one of them. As I faced each monster, they changed. As I looked at them directly and experienced them, they turned from scary, grotesque creatures into small, soft, furry little animals.

Going back and finishing each loss has taught me that it's not only okay but necessary to grieve all kinds of loss. In accepting the pain of each loss, by allowing myself to pass through each storm, I discovered that this pain is what brings growth.

My grief turned into growth in many ways. I grew into my tears and anger. As a very young child I was able to be with all my feelings the moment I had them. If I was angry I stomped my feet, screamed, yelled, and protested. If I was hurt, my tears flowed easily, but somewhere along the line I grew out of my feelings. Somehow I forgot how to be with them. I learned to shut them off in the present moment. I forgot that it is all right and important to show them. I don't know how or when all this happened. Grieving has helped me to grow back into my feelings, my tears, and my anger. Grieving has taught me not to "grow up" but to "grow down."

I've learned that it's okay to "wear my tears." When I am able to wear my tears, show my sadness, that frees other people to respond and share the tears from their similar feelings and experiences. It provides a connection for me to other human beings. In this moment we come together in our humanness, sharing with one another.

My tears are healing. They seem to cleanse the deep wound caused by loss. Their release seems to gradually lighten the load. My tears feel safe and healing.

Anger and guilt about loss are normal reactions. I discovered that if I held them inside, if I didn't let them out, they became bitter and poisonous. Freeing them, releasing the bitterness, seemed to make my tears sweeter, softer. Sometimes I forget to remember that.

I'm growing into owning all my feelings as a creative, valuable part of myself. To hide them away from myself is to hide my humanness. Owning my feelings, allowing them for myself, has put me in touch with the life force inside. In accepting the feelings of loss, I've connected with a central part of me that is caring, supportive, and nurturing to me.

In grieving, I have stumbled upon the power of choice. I am not powerless when something or someone close to me is taken away. I still have something left, as devastated as I feel; I still have the power of choice. I can choose to get with my power, which is my feelings. I can choose to accept the feelings of loss, to go through them and eventually come out the other end into the clearing where I realize the gains. Or I can choose to lock my pain away, storing it somewhere in my body, pretending it will go away, burying a part of myself, my humanness, running away from life, existing as a half instead of being whole. My personal power lies in my choices. Each choice has a price. Each costs something. Choosing to accept the pain costs agony and hurt. Choosing to run eventually causes agony and hurt, too, in the form of illness and emotional distress. For me, the pain of acceptance is the lower price.

Through grieving I've become more in touch with my body. My feelings live in my gut, they live in my body. I no longer live from the head up. I feel my entire body. I live in my entire body. I've come to understand the wisdom of my body. If I have a sore back, my body is telling me that I'm storing anger. If my chest tightens, there is hurt being locked inside. If my jaw is clenched, I'm choking back feelings. If I get a pain in the neck, someone or something ha irritated me and I'm holding onto it. Headaches tell me that I'm trying to pack my bags and move into my head again, that there's an attempt to escape the feelings that I'm pushing down and avoiding. I've learned that my body is wise. It sends me signals to remind me not to forget. It's become a special part of me. Regaining my body is teaching me about nurturing myself. I never knew what that meant before—nurturing, taking care of myself. I always thought that you did that for everybody else. I didn't understand that it's an important gift to give yourself. Nurturing myself is a lot like being a mother, only it's about being a mother to myself—doing for myself all those nice things that my mother did for me when I was a child. Like giving myself nourishment, feeding myself good nutritious foods, freeing my body up with strenuous exercise, affirming myself, telling me what a neat person I am, avoiding laying negatives and "shoulds" on myself. Taking care of myself means doing something about the messages that my body is giving me. It means expressing the feelings that I'm storing up. It means caring about me enough to risk to tell people how I feel, to let them know when I'm angry or hurt, not to get something from them, but for me, to free the tension in my body. It means nurturance in the form of rest, slowing down when my body lets me know that I'm speeding, rocking fatigue and tensions away in my rocking chair. It means taking the time to do my yoga and getting a good night's sleep after I've knotted my body up from typing for eight hours straight. Nurturance, for me, also means meeting all my needs by reaching out and asking for support and care from others when I need it. Sometimes I forget to remember.

My relationships have become deeper and richer as a result of growing through grief. Sharing my feelings, my humanity with other special people, I am touching and being touched. When I can come from a place of wholeness, I have more to give and the more I give, the more I get back. Allowing myself to feel, I can also allow the presents that other people offer to be taken in.

Grieving is teaching me to freefall. I'm learning to trust my intuition to just go with the process that is happening to me, to not judge or analyze, but just be where I am, doing what I need to do for myself.

Little by little I'm learning to unzip—to show more of me, to cease censorship on which parts of me I'll show to which people.

I've found that I have more heart. Being with my feelings of loss makes it all right for me to be there and hear other people who are going through the storm. Their tears, anguish, anger, and guilt are safe with me. I can feel with them. I can *be* with them.

I've grown through my storms of grief. But don't be seduced into thinking that I have it all together. That's not true. At times when I remember the things I've learned through grief, I'm together, centered with it. But many times, getting caught in the motion of my normal daily routines, I plug back into the illusions that I'm not going to die, that I am immune to loss. Sometimes, I forget. I don't remember what I know to be the reality.

Grief teaches, and through its lessons, life became translucent. And that allowed me to see the whole notion of loss and gain in a different light.

# THE TRANSFORMATION
# OF LOSS AND GAIN

With grief as our teacher and armed with the wisdom gained in our passage through its many lessons, our vision can change and we can begin to see loss and its other side, gain, surrounded by a different aura.

In Chapter Two we examined the concept of the t'ai chi—the essence of the circle, or whole, being its polar opposites: light and dark, female and male, loss and gain. Change was viewed as the continuous flow of one polar opposite into the other and back again. We pictured within the whole the complete circle, the seeds of the polar opposites existing concurrently. How does this perspective of the *whole* relate to the storm of grief?

In Eastern thought, life is seen through the window of this circle. Loss and gain are pictured as one, as a complete whole, one circle within the larger circle of life. Buddhist and Taoist philosophies speak about being in a dimension of no attachment, being apart from "things" and illusions. In these views, everything on the earthly plane exists in time and space. Time passes and so all things in time will also pass. Thus, nothing is permanent. All that there is is the constant flow of change, the movement of one opposite into the next, revolving back once more to the first. They speak of letting go of being attached to the idea of permanence, because this notion is an illusion. Their vision of the world is one of the unity of all things under the sun, rather than the dualities of life. Instead of focusing on the separateness of the dualities—how loss and gain, pain and pleasure, light and dark, are different from each other—they step far enough back to change the perspective and take in the entire picture. Gazing at the circle, they see the way in which the dualities are one. Their version is one of interrelatedness of all things in the universe. Contemplating the oneness of the opposites, pain and pleasure, human beings and nature, loss and gain, the illusion of permanence is transcended.

Loss and gain, death and rebirth are themes that are inherent in nature. One circle within another circle. Human beings, as part of the whole of nature, have the same themes threaded throughout their lives. Loss and gain are part of nature, so they are also within the cycle of human nature.

Loss and gain are one. These opposites comprise the whole. It is difficult at first glance to understand how two opposites can be the same. And yet we've all experienced brief moments of their unity. When was the last time that you laughed so hard it hurt? That experience is pain and pleasure as one. Have you ever had a massage that hurt so bad it felt good? That is duality as one. Loss and gain are one, they are the whole, and this perspective relates to grief. Grief, the pain of loss, is the corridor that connects loss and gain. Be-ing in the storm of grief unites loss and gain. Be-ing with the storm transcends the duality. Becoming the storm gets us with the loss, the pain, and also with the gain, the pleasure. Be-ing with the storm of grief, be-ing in the oneness of the dualities becomes a natural process, a bittersweet flow, like nature's thunderstorm.

Transcending the dualities of loss and gain enables us to accept and pass through the storm of grief, experiencing both the pain and loss and the sweetness of the gains. Being with the oneness does not magically dispel the hurt of loss, but it brings acceptance of the pain, the willingness to embrace it and pass through it via a softer path. Being with the oneness enables us to move easier with the healing process of grief because we are in harmony with the flowing of loss and gain and gain and loss. This harmony carries us toward wholeness and balance as our life reshapes itself following the loss.

Remaining tied to the illusion of permanence, we avoid and deny the fact of loss. As the reality of loss touches our life and smashes through the wall of illusion, we are caught totally unprepared. We are scared; we don't know what to do. We feel the need to run and hide—clinging, clutching this illusion, we feel powerless, defeated, and betrayed as the reality forces itself upon us. Frozen within the illusion all we see is loss, all we feel is its devastation, trapping and confusing us in its pain.

Allowing the illusion, that everything in life is permanent, to drop away frees us to accept loss and gain as a part of life. Being freed so we can accept the pain of loss as it comes opens us also to the experiences of gain, permitting us to feel, express, and release the pain, anger, and guilt that are a part of our human reaction to loss. Within this we are gently guided back toward the wholeness and unity inside.

Loss and gain are one complete circle that exists within another circle, the circle of life. Letting that reality be—that loss and gain are contained continually within the circle of life—allowing that circle to revolve unencumbered through our life is to truly live, experiencing the wholeness of life with both its light and dark sides. Being afraid of loss because we are blind to its gains, fighting it, denying it, is to condemn ourselves to pain and darkness, shutting away its gain and pleasure. Instead of unfolding with life, we become frozen within it, within ourselves, alone, terrified, cold, afraid to open and reach out, afraid to risk and afraid to live.

Within the circle of my losses, I've been given some priceless gems. In my losses I've discovered my body and we've grown to be friends. A precious part of me, my feelings, came out of loss. Within loss, I've gained deeper, richer relationships. I came to recognize real strength as being choice. My losses changed through the raging and hurt to silky softness as I gained the gift of sensitivity. Where there is gain, there is loss. And where there is loss, there is gain.

Within grief there lie both the regret of loss and the seeds of growth.

## GROWING THROUGH GRIEF

Grief contains within it the seeds of growth and enrichment. For the seeds to germinate, we need the fourth ingredient in the formula for living with loss. This is opening.

### What Is Opening?

Opening is gentle acceptance of all that is. It is a time of flowering. Just as the blossom freely receives the morning sunlight, delicately reaching its petals forth, showing itself to the world, it accepts life.

Opening is risking. It is exposing ourselves to the world, risking the threat of hurt and rejection. Opening is risking and playing with the unknown.

Opening is spreading wide our arms and hearts, taking in all that is within and without. It is still, deep water, receptive to all that is in it and around it—the blooming lilypads and the slithering snakes, the fragile butterflies and the horned toads.

Opening is the golden goblet that freely and readily receives the deep red wine of what tomorrow brings.

Opening is the gentle acceptance of all that grief brings—the howling storm of loss and the shimmering pearls of gain. It is accepting, receiving, and expanding. For the seeds to grow, we must open.

### Creating a Climate for Opening

To create a climate for opening, we must till the soil, preparing the way for the seeds to grow. Ways to nourish the soil so the seeds can put down strong, sturdy roots are freeing the child in us, freeing our feelings, and freeing the present moment.

## Freeing the Child in Us

True opening has to do with touching and freeing the child that we each carry around inside. The wound of loss touches this little child. And it is he or she who holds the feelings and has the capability to help us heal. As we pass through the storm it is important to allow this child expression. This child is about three or four years old. It is the child we were long ago—the child who was not afraid to stomp and scream when angry and wail openly when hurt, the child who knew how to *be* in the present moment, the child who displayed vulnerability with ease and openness. Become again that child who could trust feelings, who allowed their natural expression, who did not censor thoughts or feelings but unashamedly blurted them out. Become again that innocent child who was unconcerned about how others saw us, who didn't bother to make judgments about weakness or strength. Become again that child who knew instinctively how to just be, who knew how to feel whatever feelings were present in each moment. Allow that child to *be* again in grief, and allow that to be okay. Freeing the child in us opens us to ourselves. As we open to ourselves, we meet our feelings.

## Freeing our Feelings

Freeing our feelings is learning to get in touch with what we feel, owning up to it and then expressing it. Let's look at getting in touch.

Most of us, by the time we've reached adulthood, have grown out of the ability to *be with* our feelings. Most of us don't really know *how* to be with our feelings, at least not comfortably. How does this happen? We're born knowing how to feel. Most of us came into the world with great gusto and feeling. A baby cries when it's hurt and screams out in protest when it is angry. We know when young children are joyful. It radiates from head to toe. They jump up and down and dance in delight. They seem to light up with feeling. We were all like that once. But somehow, through the socialization process, our natural ability to be with our feelings got squeezed out of us. Somewhere, we learned to hide our tears, to swallow our anger, to stifle our joy. Most of us need to learn how to get *back* in touch. We're out of touch, out of touch with ourselves. We need to cut the bonds and free those feelings once again. Since feelings live inside our bodies, one of the most direct ways for finding and touching them is through the body. We need to listen to the wisdom that lies there.

Our bodies send us messages. They let us know what we're feeling. We need only listen. We've all made the remark, "He gives me a pain in the neck." That is our body telling us that we feel angry or annoyed with that person and that anger is being stowed away in our neck. We've all felt a "lump" in our throat, or "frozen" in fear, or "choked up," or we've "swallowed" our pride. The language reflects the way in which our bodies speak to us.

Our bodies send us messages. When our eyes glaze over with tears and our throats constrict, our body is telling us that we are hurt. I've heard it said that a cold is a body's way of showing unexpressed tears. When we get the message that we are feeling something, we need to get in touch with what the feeling is. A way of getting in touch is through the Physical Inventory Exercise that follows. This exercise is designed to allow you to take an inventory of what feelings you hold in different parts of your body. When we get an ache or pain or tension there, identification of that feeling will be easier. The exercise will help us to discover messages that different parts of our body may be trying to send.

**Physical Inventory.** On a separate piece of paper, list the parts of your body where you have experienced tension, tightness or pain.

Now look at each body part that has a checkmark. What feeling do you associate with that body part? When that body part is holding tension or tightness, what feeling is being stored there? Allow whatever comes to your mind to happen. Go with it, whether it is a word, image, or picture.

Record what comes to mind under the heading "Feelings."

Are there any messages that these parts of your body are sending you? Go back to the marked parts and ask. Record any messages below.

What have you learned from this inventory?

What feelings are you in touch with?

How might you use this exercise to keep yourself in touch with feelings?

This exercise is to put us in touch with our feelings so that we can begin to open to grief. Once we've allowed ourselves to *feel* the feelings, we need to *own* them. The facilitation of our tears, anger, and guilt clears the path toward owning. It is permitting whatever we're feeling to be okay. It's essentially validating ourselves by giving the message, "Hey, it's all right to feel what I'm feeling. I'm angry and that's okay." By validating our feelings we validate ourselves and move to their expression.

Once the feelings have been felt and owned, there is the need to *express* them. Having expressed them within ourselves, the time comes to reach out and express them with others. By reaching out, we allow other people in. We allow their caring and tenderness to touch us, to hug us. Having a support system—many people who are willing and able to give us what we need—is the path toward reaching out. But first, we have to nurture the ability to reach out that is a part of that child that lives inside. We have to be willing to reach out and ask for what we need. In order to do this we have to be in touch with the innocent trusting of the child within us. We have to allow the child within to show vulnerability and hurt. And we have to allow those feelings to flow out from our child within to others outside.

Then we can begin to build a support system. We need to build that community of people before loss strikes so they will already be a solid part of our lives. Creating a support system is basically setting up a group of people who will listen, accept, and allow us to share feelings. This has to be done by being selective, by choosing to allow into our lives special people with special qualities, people who have learned how to share and listen, people who don't run from tears, anger, or guilt. We need to choose people who have the ability to validate feelings, who allow us the space to be wherever we really *are*. The support system has to include a number of people. That way one person doesn't become drained. We need all the caring we can get. Obtaining this from ten people, we get more for ourselves than trying to get it all from one person. Build a community—a supportive, safe community of people who can touch and be touched. We need not allow ourselves to get trapped into the "I can't share this, I'll become a burden" syndrome. That is just a smokescreen for "I'm afraid to reach out because I might be hurt." When I discover that dialogue going on inside, I try to refocus and change the dialogue. How do I feel when someone trusts me enough to give me their feelings? I feel as if I've been handed a present. So these people who are close to me—don't they *deserve* the gift I can give them? The answer is always yes. Coming from this framework, I get around my fear and take the risk of reaching out.

Freeing our feelings is about getting in touch with them, owning them, and expressing them. Freeing our feelings opens us to ourselves and to others.

### Freeing the Present Moment

Freeing the present helps to keep us in constant touch with our feelings, so that we don't lose contact with ourselves and closeness with other people. In freeing the present, we are learning to be in the here and now with our feelings, expressing them as they bubble up. In this way we keep things clear. We don't walk around carrying the unfinished business of unexpressed feelings, clouding ourselves and our relationships. The way to free the present is to share and express feelings as they come up, rather than to stuff them down or hold them inside. It is when we directly and honestly communicate feelings, *as we feel them,* in the now moment. To express the feelings of now, begin by using an "I" statement. That is, start out by saying "I feel." Then put in the feeling. "I feel uptight right now." "I feel put-down, and I don't like it." "I'm excited." The idea is to be in touch with our feelings as they change, to *own* them, and to express them as they occur. In this way, spontaneous expression becomes a natural, flowing part of us. In this way, we keep the present free and clear. We're not carrying around extra baggage. Freeing the present opens us to the now moment. Being in the now moment, we experience richness and quality. Freeing the present opens us to ourselves, to others, and to life.

To create opening, we need to free the child that lives inside us, to free our feelings, and to free the present moment.

Opening is the ingredient that leads us to the clearing, to the other side of grief. It is in opening ourselves to grief—by accepting its dark side of pain and hurt and its light side of lessons and gifts—that we come to the clearing. Opening to the total experience of grief, all that it has to give, the loss and the gains, is how we grow through grief.

## WHAT DOES IT MEAN TO LIVE WITH LOSS

Loss intrudes upon our world, disrupting it, sending jagged pieces of it bursting out in all directions. And we are left behind shaken and frightened and torn. How do we survive this devastation? How do we put it all back together? And what does it mean to live with loss?

### How Do We Survive Loss?

Understanding that loss is a natural part of the wheel of life helps us to turn toward it and encounter it. Seeing loss through the framework of nature's summer storm, thunder as loss, the storm as the journey through grief, the mire as grief when it is stalled, and the clearing as its other side of renewal and gain—all of this will bring us toward that understanding.

To open ourselves to experience and travel through our grief is the way we survive loss. Using the formula with its four basic ingredients is the way we open. Intrinsically threaded together, these components are interdependent, being as one. None of them stands alone. All are a part that, together, make up the whole. Permission, trust, flow, and opening—all make up the whole. The whole is our journey through grief. By giving ourselves permission, we accept loss and its staggering feelings and pass through thunder and lightning. Trust enables us to *affirm* the feelings, which in turn allows us to *feel* them and *express* them. This moves us toward and through the storm. Flow moves with the feelings and whisks us past the mire. And opening, which is made possible by permission, trust, and flow, brings us into the clearing. Together, as a whole they are our journey through grief to its other side. Journeying through our grief is how we live with loss.

Living with loss means feeling it, experiencing it. It means being coura geous enough to surrender to the storm, to feel it, express it, and let it go. In letting go, we can again reach the clearing, learn, grow, and once again risk; we can give our hearts away in the knowledge that we will again lose. And within this loss we will gain and eventually lose again.

Living with loss means embracing the circle of life. Living with loss means allowing, affirming, flowing, and opening to life. It means dancing with all of life—its gains and its losses.

# Notes

## CHAPTER ONE: THUNDER AND LIGHTNING

[1] Richard Wilhelm, trans., *The I Ching or Book of Changes* (Princeton, N. J.: Princeton University Press, 1967), pp. 1v-1vi.

[2] D. Peretz, "Development, Object Relationships and Losses," in *Loss and Grief: Psychological Management in Medical Practice,* ed. B. Shoenberg, A. Carr, D. Peretz, and A. Kutscher (New York: Columbia University Press, 1970), p. 5.

[3] Alexander Lowen, M. D., *Depression and the Body: The Biological Basis of Faith and Reality* (New York: Coward, McCann & Geohegan, Inc., 1973), p. 132.

[4] Ibid., p. 132.

[5] Ibid., p. 132.

[6] Lilly Pincus, *Death and the Family: The Importance of Mourning* (New York: Random House, Inc., 1976), p. 128.

[7] Lowen, *Depression and the Body,* pp. 133-34.

[8] John Bowlby, "Childhood Mourning: Its Implication for Psychiatry," *The American Journal of Psychiatry,* 118, (December 1961), 481-97.

[9] Quoted from Pincus, *Death and the Family,* p. 129.

[10] D. Peretz, "Development, Object Relationships and Losses, in *Loss and Grief: Psychological Management in Medical Practice,* ed. B. Shoenberg, A. Carr, D. Peretz, and A. Kutscher (New York: Columbia University Press, 1970), p. 6.

[11] Melba Colgrove, Ph.D., Harold H. Bloomfield, M.D., and Peter McWilliams, *How To Survive The Loss of a Love* (New York: Bantam Books, Inc., 1977), pp. 3-7.

# CHAPTER TWO: THE STORM

[1] Colin Murray Parkes, *Bereavement: Studies of Grief in Adult Life* (New York: International Universities Press, Inc., 1972), p. 6.

[2] Edgar Jackson, *Understanding Grief: Its Roots, Dynamics and Treatment* (Nashville, Tenn. Abingdon Press, 1957), p. 18.

[3] Ira Tanner, *The Gift of Grief: Healing the Pain of Everyday Losses* (New York: Hawthorne Books, Inc., 1976), p. 157.

[4] Ira O. Glick, Robert S. Weiss, and C. Murray Parkes, *The First Year of Bereavement* (New York: A Wiley-Interscience Publication, John Wiley & Sons, 1974), p. 4.

[5] Ibid., p. 4.

[6] Ibid.

[7] Ibid.

[8] Ibid., p. 6.

[9] Ibid., p. 8.

[10] Erich Lindemann, "The Symptomology and Management of Acute Grief," in *Death and Identity*, ed. Robert Fulton (New York: Wiley & Sons, Inc., 1965) pp. 186-201.

[11] From E. Lindemann and I. Greer, "A Study of Grief: Emotional Responses to Suicide," in *Survivors of Suicide*, ed. A. Caine 1972, Courtesy of Charles C. Thomas, Publisher, Springfield, Illinois, p. 64.

[12] John Bowlby, "The Process of Mourning," *International Journal of Psycho-Analysis*, 42 1961), 317-39.

[13] Parkes, *Bereavement: Studies of Grief.*

# CHAPTER THREE: THE MIRE

[*] Jackson, *Understanding Grief*, p. 31.

[1] Eric Lindemann, "The Symptomology and Management of Acute Grief," in *Death and Identity*, ed. Robert Fulton (New York: Wiley & Sons, Inc., (1965).

[2] Ibid., p. 193.

[3] Ibid., p. 197.

[4] Colin Murray Parkes, "Seeking and Finding a Lost Object: Evidence from Recent Studies of the Reaction to Bereavement," *Social Science and Medicine*, vol 4, (1970), p. 196.

[5] Cited in N. Paul, "Psychiatry: Its Role in the Resolution of Grief," in *Death and Bereavement*, ed. A. Kutscher (Springfield, Ill.: Charles C. Thomas, 1967) p. 181.

[6] H. Stone, *Suicide and Grief* (Philadelphia: Fortress Press, 1972), p. 32.

[7] Elisabeth Kübler-Ross, *On Death and Dying*, Copyright © 1969 by Elizabeth Kübler-Ross. New York: Macmillan Publishing Co., Inc., 1969; London: Tavistock Publications Ltd., 1970), p. 271.

[8] O. Carl Simonton, M.D., Stephanie Matthews-Simonton, and James L. Creighton, *Getting Well Again* (New York: Bantam Books, 1980).

[9] Ibid., p. 62.

[10] Ibid., p. 63.

[11] Ibid., p. 79.

[12] Ibid.

[13] Ibid.

[14] Ibid.

[15] Ibid., pp. 56-57.

[16] In Kenneth Pelletier, *Mind As Healer, Mind As Slayer: A Holistic Approach to Preventing Stress Disorders* (New York: Delacorte Press/Seymour Lawrence, 1977), p. 137.

[17] Cited in Simonton et al., *Getting Well Again*, p. 45.

[18] Ibid., p. 63.

[19] O. Goldfarb, J. Drieson, and D. Cole, "Psychophysiologic Aspects of Malignancy," *American Journal of Psychiatry*, 123 (June 1967), 1545-51.

[20] Pelletier, *Mind As Healer*, p. 137.

[21] Ibid., p. 150.

[22] M. Young, B. Benjamin, and C. Wallis, "The Mortality of Widows," *Lancet*, 2 (1963).

[23] Ibid., p. 456.

[24] Lilly Pincus, *Death and the Family: The Importance of Mourning* (New York: Random House, Inc., 1976), p. 259.

[25] Helen A. DeRosis, M.D. and Victoria Y. Pellegrino, *The Book of Hope: How Women Can Overcome Depression* (New York: Macmillan Publishing Co., Inc., 1976), pp. 31-32. Copyright © 1976 by Helen A. DeRosis and Victoria Y. Pellegrino.

[26] Pincus, *Death and the Family*, pp. 182-83.

[27] Kübler-Ross, *On Death and Dying*, p. 110.

[28] DeRosis and Pellegrino, *The Book of Hope*, p. 32.

[29] Pincus, *Death and the Family*, p. 179.

[30] DeRosis and Pellegrino, *The Book of Hope*, p. 160.

[31] Ibid.

[32] T. Dorpat, "Psychological Effects of Parental Suicide on Surviving Children," in *Survivor of Suicide*, ed. A. Caine (Springfield, Ill.: Charles C. Thomas, 1972), p. 127.

[33] Colin Murray Parkes, "Seeking and Finding a Lost Object: Evidence From Recent Studies of the Reaction To Bereavement," *Social Science and Medicine*, 4 (1970), 187-201.

[34] Edgar Jackson, *Understanding Grief: Its Roots, Dynamics and Treatment* (Nashville, Tenn.: Abingdon Press, 1957), p. 60.

[35] Stone, *Suicide And Grief*, p. 34.

[36] Parkes, *"Seeking and Finding,"* pp. 187-201.

[37] C. Anderson, "Aspects of Pathological Grief and Mourning," *International Journal of Psycho-Analysis*, 30 (1949), 48-53.

[38] Lindemann, *The Symptomology and Management of Acute Grief*, p. 197.

[39] Kenneth Pelletier, *Mind As Healer, Mind As Slayer* (New York: Delacorte Press/Seymour Lawrence, 1977), p. 140. Originally published in *Moneysworth*, May 26, 1975.

[40] M. Friedman and R. H. Rosenmann, "Type A Behavior Pattern: Its Association with Coronary Heart Disease," *Annals of Clinical Research*, 3 (1971), 300-12.

[41] Cited in Kenneth Pelletier, *Mind As Healer, Mind As Slayer* (New York: Delacorte Press/Seymour Lawrence, 1977), p. 126.

# Bibliography

Anderson, C. "Aspects of Pathological Grief and Mourning," *International Journal of Psycho-Analysis,* 30 (1949), 48-53.

Bowlby, John. "Childhood Mourning: Its Implication for Psychiatry," *The American Journal of Psychiatry,* 118 (1961), 481-97.

_____ . "Process of Mourning," *International Journal of Psycho-Analysis,* 42, (1961), 317-39.

_____ . "Pathological Mourning and Childhood Mourning," *American Psychoanalytic Association Journal,* 2 (1963), 500-41.

Carr, A. "Bereavement as a Relative Experience," in *Bereavement: Its Psychosocial Aspects,* ed. B. Shoenberg, I. Gerber, A. Wiener, A. Kutscher, D. Peretz, and A. Carr, New York: Columbia University Press, 1975.

Colgrove, M., H. Bloomfield, and P. McWilliams. *How to Survive the Loss of a Love.* New York: Bantam Books, Inc., 1977.

Dorpat, T. "Psychological Effects of Parental Suicide on Surviving Children," in *Survivors of Suicide,* ed. A. Caine. Springfield, Ill.: Charles C. Thomas, 1972.

DeRosis, Helen, and Victoria Y. Pellegrino. *The Book of Hope: How Women Can Overcome Depression.* New York: Macmillan Publishing Co., Inc., 1976.

Elliot, Thomas B. "The Bereaved Family," *Annals of the American Academy of Political and Social Science,* 160 (1932), 184-90.

Friedman, M., and R. H. Rosemann. "Type A Behavior Pattern: Its Association with Coronary Heart Disease," *Annals of Clinical Research,* 3 (1971), 300-12.

Freud, Sigmund. "Mourning and Melancholia," in *The Standard Edition of the Complete Psychological Works of Sigmund Freud,* Vol. 14, trans. J. Strachey. London: The Hogarth Press, 1953.

Fulcomer, David M. *The Adjusted Behavior of Some Recently Bereaved Spouses: A Psycho-Social Study.* Unpublished doctoral dissertation, Northwestern University, 1942.

Glick, I. O., Robert S. Weiss, and Colin Murray Parkes. *The First Year of Bereavement.* New York: John Wiley & Sons, Inc., 1974.

Goldfarb, O., J. Drieson, and D. Cole. "Psychophysiologic Aspects of Malignancy," *American Journal of Psychiatry,* 123 (June 1967), 1545-51.

Jackson, Edgar. *Understanding Grief: Its Roots, Dynamics and Treatment.* Nashville, Tenn.: Abingdon Press, 1957.

Klein, Melanie, "Mourning and Its Relationship to Manic-Depressive States," *International Journal of Psycho-Analysis,* 21 (1940), 125.

Kowal, S. J. "Emotions as a Cause of Cancer: Eighteenth and Nineteenth Century Contributions," *Psychoanalytic Review,* 42 (1955), 217-27.

Krupp, G. "The Bereavement Reaction: A Special Case of Separation Anxiety, Sociocultural Considerations," in *The Psychoanalytic Study of Society,* vol. 2, ed. W. Muensterberger and S. Axelrad. New York: International Universities Press, 1962.

Kübler-Ross, Elisabeth. *On Death and Dying.* Copyright 1969, by Elisabeth Kübler-Ross. New York: Macmillan Publishing Co., Inc., 1969.

LeShan, L. Psychological States as Factors in the Development of Malignant Disease: A Critical Review," *Journal of the National Cancer Institute,* 22 (1959), 1-18.

Lindemann, Erich. "The Symptomology and Management of Acute Grief," in *Death and Identity,* ed. Robert Fulton. New York: John Wiley & Sons, Inc., 1965.

Lindemann, Erich, and I. Greer. "A Study of Grief: Emotional Responses to Suicide," in *Survivors to Suicide,* ed. A. Caine, 1972. Courtesy of Charles C. Thomas, Publisher, Springfield, Illinois.

Lowen, Alexander. *Depression and the Body: The Biological Basis of Faith and Reality.* Baltimore, Md.: Penguin Books, Inc., 1974.

Parkes, Colin Murray. *Bereavement: Studies of Grief in Adult Life.* New York: International Universities Press, Inc., 1972.

_____. "Seeking and Finding a Lost Object: Evidence from Recent Studies of the Reaction to Bereavement," *Social Science and Medicine,* 4 (1970), 187-201.

Paul, N. "Psychiatry: Its Role in the Resolution of Grief," in *Death and Bereavement,* ed. A. Kutscher. Springfield, Ill.: Charles C. Thomas, 1969.

Pelletier, Kenneth, *Mind As Healer, Mind As Slayer: A Holistic Approach to Preventing Stress Disorders.* New York: Delacourte Press/Seymour Lawrence, 1977.

Pincus, Lilly. *Death and the Family: The Importance of Mourning.* New York: Random House, Inc., 1976.

Schoenberg, B., A. Carr, D. Peretz, and A. Kutscher, eds. *Loss and Grief: Psychological Management in Medical Practice.* New York: Columbia University Press, 1970.

Simonton, Carl O., M.D., Stephanie Matthews-Simonton, and James L. Creighton. *Getting Well Again.* New York: Bantam Books, Inc., 1980.

Stone, H. *Suicide and Grief.* Philadelphia: Fortress Press, 1972.

Tanner, Ira. *The Gift of Grief: Healing the Pain of Everyday Losses.* New York: Hawthorne Books, Inc., 1976.

# Index